GLORY DAYS

Devon General

Colin Morris

Ian Allan
PUBLISHING

Contents

First published 2006
ISBN (10) 0 7110 3128 2
ISBN (13) 978 0 7110 3128 9

Published by Ian Allan Publishing

an imprint of Ian Allan Publishing Ltd, Hersham, Surrey KT12 4RG

Printed in England by Ian Allan Printing Ltd, Hersham, Surrey KT12 4RG

Code: 0609/B1

Visit the Ian Allan Publishing website at www.ianallanpublishing.com

The impressive figure of Gerald Truran, Engineering Assistant at Devon General, shows his affection for AEC Regal III TCR629 (LTA 629) of 1950, survivor of its batch of 12. The last new half-cab coaches in the fleet, they were fitted with Duple's most attractive A-type coachwork. *Royston Morgan*

Acknowledgements

My regard for Devon as being a somewhat special place was sparked at a very early age by a photograph in the family album of my mother Elsie Lock and her sister Ethel enjoying the sunshine on Meadfoot Beach — with Thatcher Point, Thatcher Rock and the Ore Stone in the background — taken in the early 'Twenties. As young ladies they'd travelled down, by motor-cycle (!), from their home near Crewkerne, Somerset. Aunt Ethel later lived in Okehampton and Germansweek and sent me pocket guides and letters extolling the beauties of hilly Devon. I eventually went to look for myself; she was right. The West Country as a whole stimulates one's sensory perception in all its forms, but Devon . . . is indeed rather special. I've experienced great pleasure in setting foot or wheel across its borders ever since.

So, it was with considerable delight that I agreed to a request from Peter Waller of Ian Allan Publishing that I should write a book about Devon General in the 'Glory Days' series.

In 1966 Ian Allan Ltd published a 112-page history of the Devon General Omnibus & Touring Co Ltd, compiled jointly, so it was claimed, by the PSV Circle and the Omnibus Society. Closer inspection revealed that, although it was indeed compiled in that duo's vehicle-centred format, this was the work of Leslie F. Folkard — aided by such company stalwarts as Gerald Sedgwick and Gerald Truran — at a time when his father, Noel, was the company's highly regarded Tours Superintendent, based in Torquay. Les Folkard, the Devon General Society's honorary historian, has brought together in a detailed history much of what he has written over the years, and, when published, this will prove to be the definitive record of the part played by the company in the story of road transport in the West Country.

For the purpose of this short volume I have taken the liberty of identifying Devon General's 'Glory Days' as being those between 1919 and 1970, when the Devon General Omnibus & Touring Co Ltd was an active firm and before it was 'put to sleep' by the National Bus Company.

I was honoured to be invited to Marldon, near Paignton, by John 'Jack' Jarvis, who joined the company in 1939 and retired as District Manager for the later Devon General Ltd, under the

For John 'Jack' Jarvis — from conductor (1939) to District Manager, Devon General. Described by Michael Rourke as 'Devon General born and bred'.

ægis of NBC. He kindly permitted me to record his recollections of those days. This was an introduction made by Michael Rourke, Traffic Manager of Western National and, later, Managing Director of a new Southern National.

I received much help and advice from the staff of the Torquay Central Library's Reference Department and from the Devon County Record Office. My thanks go also to Susan and Royston Morgan, of Stapleford, Nottingham, for their hospitality, the latter providing a wealth of information, artefacts and illustrations from which to choose — and even an offer to drive (somewhere safe) his beautifully restored Devon General AEC Regent V. I am similarly obliged to the stalwart group now in the advanced stages of setting up that most professional and exciting project, the West Country Historic Omnibus & Transport Trust (WHOTT), at West Point, Exeter — in particular Philip Platt, Colin Shears and my helper previously with *Glory Days: Royal Blue* (2000), Robert J. Crawley. All these Devon-based gentlemen have raised the profile of this work by their advice, help and the loan of high-quality pictures.

Needless to say, my long-standing friends Andrew Waller and Alan Lambert have again weighed in with their much-valued contributions, the latter doing the navigating as we searched out the locations of the first board meetings of Devon General, both in London and in West Sussex (yes, that's correct!). And, a new one, Mallory Saltmarsh, of Cowplain, Hampshire, has surprised me with the sheer volume of his Devon General photographic collection and his generosity in permitting me to take my pick.

Finally, a big thankyou to Peter Jaques, doyen of that remarkable source of information, the Kithead Trust at Droitwich. From him, of late, I have learned to listen, rather than gabble, when advice and information is being proffered, with such classic lines as: "Just switch to 'receive' mode for a moment, Colin." All good stuff. I have truly enjoyed putting this volume together. So, if you're looking down, thank you too, Aunt Ethel.

Colin Morris
Heswall
May 2006

Horse-drawn tramways were first laid down in Exeter during 1882, three basic lines radiating from London Inn Square (which location would, some 38 years later, become the centre for Devon General's Exeter-based operations). Exeter Corporation purchased the tramways company's operation in 1902, extended and electrified it, purchasing an initial 12 Dick, Kerr cars, ready for an April 1905 opening ceremony.
Soon after, one of these cars (No 9), bound for Heavitree, passes the oldest Guildhall in Britain as a carpenter's assistant crosses the road with his gluepot.
Colin Morris collection

Anyone familiar with the numbering process associated with the identity of limited-liability companies would be mildly surprised to discover that the official company number of Arriva Cymru Ltd (whose registered office is . . . no, not in Wales, but in Sunderland, Tyne & Wear) is 155374. The computer at Companies House will tell you that the date of incorporation of this company was 22 May 1919, and under 'Previous Names' is listed just one — 'Crosville Wales Ltd'. Which goes to show that computers are only as good as the basic information they are given in the first place. What has that got to do with the subject of this book? Well, the clue lies with the given date of incorporation, but more upon this later.

So, on to seemingly more appropriate territory — that of a heady admixture: magnificent fertile valleys, imposing hills, a coastline interspersed with the charming and the awe-inspiring, beautiful streams and rivers, enchanting villages and towns, the ancient city of Exeter — and the not-so-old 'English Riviera' resort of Torquay. In other words, the area once served by a characterful omnibus company called 'Devon General'. Or, as the descendants of the original Celtic/Saxon inhabitants of the area pronounced it, 'Deb'n Gen'ral'. And, if the capital of England had remained in Winchester, rather than move to London, we'd all have pronounced it that way.

To the south-west of Exeter the steep hills and 'deep valleys' which gave Devon its name begin in earnest. As a result the Romans, with their predilection for building straight roads, seem to have faltered somewhat in their march westward. Small wonder, for as late as 1968 the Royal Automobile Club listed 94 challenging roads in Devon with a maximum gradient of 1 in 5 or worse — more than twice the number in Yorkshire, the second county in Great Britain so encumbered. Such terrain, greatly attractive to tourists, nevertheless proved a considerable test for horse-drawn traffic and the earliest of motor vehicles which followed; even those which emerged modestly triumphant enjoyed comparatively short lives to those elsewhere.

This, then, was why Devon, in particular, was rather late to enjoy the attentions of emergent territorial bus companies in the early 20th century. Until reliable equipment came on stream it just wasn't profitable enough to attract them. To a large extent the development of passenger transport in the area had been left to locally based 19th-century pioneers who'd found a limited number of routes which would not prove too demanding for their horses.

Exeter, relatively flat and accessible from the east, had enjoyed a stage- and mail-coach service to London whose reputation rivalled that on the London–Bath road. There was an established trade built around the provision of horses for such traffic, so that when I. K. Brunel's railway arrived in the city several proprietors found themselves able to provide local services focussed upon the main railway stations. These sufficed until, in 1877, there was an abortive attempt to establish a horse-drawn tramway service in Exeter. Eight subscribers, including four merchants, two JPs and Edward Harris, Headmaster of Exeter Grammar School, founded Company No 11897, the Exeter Tramways Company, which was incorporated on 13 December 1877. This version of ETC, however, never did carry on any business and was dissolved on 3 September 1886. Meanwhile, in 1880, Messrs Moore, Bidder and Buckland set out to establish a company of exactly the same name* — and succeeded where the original failed. Well, to a certain extent: it survived nearly being wound up in 1883, to be run — in concert with a group of local horse-bus proprietors — by The Tramway Purchase Syndicate.

In 1903 what remained of this small system was acquired by Exeter Corporation, extended to some five miles of route and electrified. Such, then, were the origins of the City of Exeter Transport Department. For 67 years afterward public transport here would be under the control of local councillors.

Before moving south to consider the Torbay area it is perhaps appropriate to look at the area to the west and south-west of Exeter. During the first decade of the 20th century (in 1907, for instance) there were three public-service routes between Exeter and Chagford (an historic village set beside scenery of charm and outstanding beauty):

* I'm not sure how that was possible; there's room for some more research here, but the details are not in the National Archives

1) London & South Western Railway motor bus the whole way — 21 miles — in 2hr 15min for 2s 6d (12½p);
2) Great Western Railway train to Newton Abbot and thence to Moretonhampstead and on by GWR motor bus — 37 miles — in 3hr 30min for 3s 5½d (c17p);
3) GWR train to Moreton by GWR-sponsored Exeter Railway and thence by GWR motor bus — 30 miles — in 3hr 50min for 2s 10½d (c14p).

Running on the seemingly standard West Country gauge of 3ft 6in, Exeter Corporation Tramways operated nearly five miles of route, until 1931, from its depot on the south side of Paris Street. Initially dark green and cream, the former was replaced c1925 by a lighter Napier green. From that time some cars were 'vestibuled', with three windows around each end to provide weather-protection for the driver, No 27 being an example. Replacement buses began to enter service in 1929: some 16 years later Devon General was destined to become deeply involved in that operation.
Colin Morris collection

Among the early operators of motor omnibuses in the area to which the Devon General Omnibus & Touring Co Ltd would later lay claim was the London & South Western Railway Co. Despite the rather misleading board (along the luggage rack) advertising the LSWR's rail route from London to Plymouth, this 16hp Milnes-Daimler (A 4284) was one of a pair which established a route between Exeter and Chagford on 1 June 1904.
Colin Morris collection

The LSWR motor bus was thus the
best bet.

So, in August 1907, Exeter Railway
directors came up with a scheme for
'The Fingle Glen Motor Track' along part
of the Teign Valley, connecting the road
near Dunsford with that on the approach
to Chagford. The plan was reported
in all seriousness in the journal *Motor
Traction*. The track was to be laid upon
concrete foundations, with cast metal
trays to guide the wheels of the buses and
lorries it was decided should use it. The
account does not say whether it was to be
a dual carriageway, to permit vehicles to
pass in opposite directions, nor what
would happen if a vehicle broke down in
the trays, or water turned to ice in them.

◄ Probably preoccupied with setting up a bus operation in the Torbay area, the Great Western Railway Co did not serve Chagford until 1906. The LSWR Clarksons having repeatedly proved in need of remedial work, they were replaced in May 1908 by a pair of 24hp Thornycroft saloon buses (AA 2235/6) with 16-seat Hora bodywork. They served on the Exeter–Chagford route until the outbreak of World War 1. *Colin Morris collection*

This surely unworkable scheme was proposed as a fourth method of travelling between Exeter and Chagford (estimated figures: Exeter Railway train to Christow and thence by GWR motor bus along the 'motor track' — a total distance of 20 miles — in 1hr 20 minutes for 2s 3d [11p]). The scheme was possibly inspired by the early-19th-century granite tramway on Hay Tor, designed to bring stone down from the quarries. Whatever, it did not get beyond the paper stage.

The GWR ('the cat that walked alone') proved even less interested in that idea than it had many years before in atmospheric railways, such as I. K. Brunel had constructed experimentally between Exeter and Newton Abbot; the best-laid schemes . . . mice (and rats) ate the leather propellant airbags to bring that to a standstill. And in neither case were Devonshire pixies responsible.

Whilst Exeter is historically ancient, Torquay as we know it is a comparative concoction, founded directly as a result of Napoleon Bonaparte's lengthy attempt by force of arms to establish a 'Greater France' across Europe. Thus deprived of their annual visits to the French Riviera, the wealthy from anywhere but Devon discovered what senior officers of the Royal Navy had already found: a small fishing village facing south over Torbay, whose sheltered position and health-giving climate offered the alternative they sought — a viable 'English' Riviera. It was probably the Navy, whose ships paraded across the safe anchorage of Torbay in three neat ranks, that planted the original New Zealand cordylines now proliferating in the area (and which residents and visitors alike are happy to pretend are palm trees). The sailors, re-victualling their ships in Torbay, witnessed the final act of the Napoleonic War in July 1815, when Bonaparte

Torquay, as we know it, was developed as a result of Napoleon Bonaparte's antics across the continent of Europe. Deprived of access to the French Riviera, wealthy folk from beyond Devon built themselves villas where once sheep and goats had grazed. Torquay's arms commemorate the Navy's use of Torbay, culminating in HMS *Bellerophon*'s arrival with Napoleon aboard as a prisoner and temporary tourist attraction — right there, just off 'his' Torquay, 'England's Riviera'.
Colin Morris collection

Some idea of what the coastline of that part of Torquay which faces Torbay looked like in the early part of the 19th century — before developers 'removed' the original Devon folk from the south-facing part of the headland — may be gained from this 1930s view of Torquay's Oddicombe Beach. In the left foreground is the lower station of Babbacombe Cliff Railway, at one time operated by Torquay Tramways.
Colin Morris collection

himself, a prisoner aboard HMS *Bellerophon*, sailed up to the anchorage. As *Bellerophon* hove to near Thatcher Rock, Napoleon gazed at 'his' Torquay. "What a beautiful country!" he exclaimed — and few have disagreed with him since. But even this accolade did not win him permission to go ashore — which is just as well, because he would have had us driving on the wrong side of the road and using metric measurements in no time. Instead, he briefly became Torquay's first tourist attraction as boatloads were rowed out to watch him pacing the deck.

When the Navy left Torbay the speculators moved in. The rocky hills of Torquay were divided up into two-acre plots, for sale as sites for the elegant

villas which — perched upon their crags and converted into hotels — today give Torquay its spectacular appeal. What happened to the indigenous Devon folk who previously lived there? Well, the amazing opening paragraph of *The Torbay Household & Business Directory* for 1911/12 tells us in no uncertain fashion: 'Torquay is the principal watering place and residential town in the West of England. There are no manufactories, and the object of the municipality is to attract people to reside in the town . . . no less than £60,000 having within recent years been expended in purchasing the whole of the watershed and removing every farm and other human habitation from its surface . . . it is doubtful if any other town has taken the precaution of sweeping away the population — and thus making the water absolutely free from pollution.' No, indeed; they played it straight at Torquay in those days!

The Navy's unwitting part in all this is commemorated in the Torquay coat of arms, whose main motif is a three-masted fully rigged man o' war — designed, one suspects, by a reactionary native of 'proper Devon', for it is sailing to the left and flying a red flag from each masthead.

The notion of a town specially created for wealthy 'immigrants', serviced by the surviving local populace, is not unique, but it was most marked in Torquay. The theme extends historically to the provision of public transport in the area. The original horse-drawn stage-carriage services and touring facilities were provided by genuine 'Devon folk'. As suggested earlier, when advances in technology made it viable so the major providers and financial backers of road transport for the area came from without — as did their senior officers on site. Again, this is far from unique, but it was to prove noticeably so throughout the history of the Devon General Omnibus & Touring Co Ltd.

From 1848 local proprietors had provided horse-drawn buses from Torre station, along the flatter stretches of road. They went largely unsupervised, for the Torquay Local Board, forerunner of the Corporation, was not founded until 1850, when the population stood at 11,500. As the railway advanced towards a terminus at Kingswear the local proprietors focused on Torquay station, forming themselves into the Torquay Omnibus Association, but this had collapsed by 1859. Thus progress was a thing of fits and starts, so the first properly timetabled omnibus service between Torquay and Paignton did not commence until June 1872. There was at that time in Union Street, Torquay, a long line of up to eight omnibuses which jostled each other for custom at all hours of the day. Deprived of an association, by 1885 they had gone to the wall; there were then just four-seat cabs and one antique box-on-wheels which did duty as an omnibus.

Indicative of the constraints imposed by the local terrain is that a seven-seat MMC wagonette, introduced in November 1898 by the London Motor Van & Wagon Co Ltd to run at Torquay, lasted less than a year.

The tractive effort achievable with steam propulsion was to prove more effective in tackling the hills, but a LIFU placed in service by Thomas Adams in 1899 to run between Paignton and Torquay seems to have been confined to the comparatively level run along the shoreline of Torbay. Things began to look up somewhat in 1903 with the introduction of the first locally run Clarkson steam bus — a manufacturer destined to be well represented in the area for the best part of a decade afterward.

The original (T46) and seven others which followed were placed in service by the Torquay & District Motor Omnibus Co Ltd, of Market Street — a syndicate under the chairmanship of William Callard, a baker and confectioner of 162/164 Union Street and other local outlets.

This company was operative for three years, but no sooner had it started than the directors got wind of the newly founded Torquay Tramways Co Ltd and its plans to dig up the roads in the area in order to install the necessary trackwork.

The T&DMOC directors got out of the business whilst the going was good and, in February 1907, sold its buses to the Harrogate Road Car Co Ltd — the shareholders discovering to their surprise that they were to receive all their money back, plus a final bonus of 9%. Not all agreed with this move, and some of the ex-T&DMOC shareholders formed the Torquay Road Car Co Ltd, again with Clarkson steam buses but all second-hand — two from Eastbourne Corporation, plus a body from the Great Western Railway, and three from the Vale of Llangollen Engineering, Bus & Garage Co Ltd — two of which had previously served with the Sussex Motor Road Car Co in the Worthing area.

From the quay where the monks of Torre Abbey shipped their products and landed their supplies was developed a fishing port and then a harbour for leisure pursuits. On a turn-of-the-century Regatta Day in Torquay Harbour a lone one-horse landau approaches Princess Gardens some seven years before tramways were constructed in the town.
Colin Morris collection

Although this photograph was taken in the early 20th century (the Mallock Memorial Clock Tower is in place) the tramlines have not yet been laid. From the bay in the foreground the road is riven by the marks left by departing hackney carriages, whose station was at this point. A passenger-less one-horse landau approaches the bay whilst a two-horse brake enters the Strand.
Colin Morris collection

Travel by road carriage beyond the relatively flat coast road around Torbay required at least two horses per vehicle. Among the jobmasters and carriage proprietors who provided the latter were R. H. Grist and W. E. Cawdle. Whereas at most other seaside locations fanciful fleetnames were employed, both used simply their surnames, as upon this 18-seat charabanc of Cawdle, whose operation later became the local 'Royal Blue'.
Colin Morris collection

In July 1904 the Great Western Railway's Road Motor Department placed two 20hp Milnes-Daimler motor buses in service on the Paignton–Torquay road. Originally intended for service at Helston, No 20 (A 6181) was a rear-entrance 19-seat wagonette with an unusual rear-mounted nearside ladder giving access to its near-full-length roof rack.
Alan Lambert collection

Since early petrol-engined vehicles were of low power and therefore of little use in hilly Devon the steam-powered omnibus was seen as an answer, and this form of traction was to prove quite popular in the Torbay area for over a decade. The first local proprietor to try it for passenger-carrying service was Thomas Adams, who in 1899 placed this LIFU in service between Paignton and Torquay.
Colin Morris collection

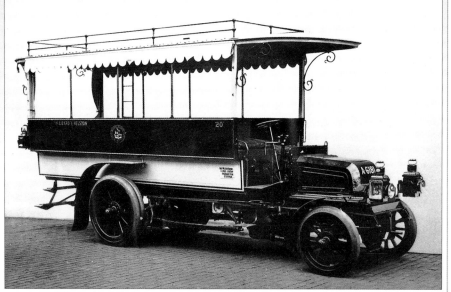

The TRCC scratched a living along the coast road to Paignton, not yet served by trams. It did not, however, do too well there; that route had been bagged by the first of 'the outsiders' — the Road Motor Department of the Great Western Railway — as early as 11 July 1904. Starting in the Torbay area humbly enough, with two Milnes Daimlers based in Paignton, the GWR had built up a local fleet of 15 vehicles at the height of TRCC's activities, and the latter collapsed in December 1908. The GWR added two more Milnes Daimlers from the short-lived Paignton & District Motor Omnibus Co in 1910. One was DL 254, which appeared in Torquay at the same time as two others (DL 255/6) operated by George Senior, of 5 Market Street. (When new all three had possibly been earmarked for Douglas Mackenzie's 'Western Motor Coaches Ltd' of Minehead, some eight years before his participation in the founding of Southdown Motor Services Ltd at Brighton; he had registered several vehicles at Ryde for use elsewhere.) However, the GWR, like other bus operators in the area, would be obliged to retreat in the face of the establishment of a tramway.

There had, in 1859, been a scheme to construct a horse-drawn tramway from the harbour to the new Torquay railway station. Those plans were contemporaneous with those of George Francis Train for Birkenhead — but Torquay escaped. Another unrealised plan came forth in 1876, for a line from Torre station to Victoria Parade. Both of these routes were later covered by the second — and lasting — intruder, the National Electric Construction Co Ltd, of Laurence Pountney Hill, London; it established, in similar fashion to the Provincial group, Imperial Tramways and the British Electric Traction Co,

GWR Milnes-Daimler No 20 was licensed at the same time as Milnes-Daimler No 16, fitted with a 36-seat open-top double-deck body with open staircase. This bus was given special praise in the local press because of the splendid views from the *lower* saloon. This probably had more to do with its glazed lower sides, which protected the viewers from the sea-spray, evident here. *Alan Lambert collection*

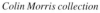

'Two little maids from school' (a popular Gilbert & Sullivan song at the time) come through the Rock Gardens toward Shedden Hill Road as GWR 24hp Milnes-Daimler No 57 (A 9755) swings along the Esplanade on a journey to Paignton *c*1906, before the tramlines were laid. On a sunny summer's day such as this a trip around the bay on the top deck must have been an exciting experience for locals and visitors alike. *Colin Morris collection*

The Great Western Railway seems to have had body-swapping facilities available at its Paignton premises, for when Torquay Tramways began operating (from 1907), chassis No 57 (A 9755) turned up ready for excursions and tours business in the area. Devon was clearly enjoying more sunny weather — the 'well-heeled' barefoot boy with panama hat looks suitably prepared.
Alan Lambert collection

Torquay Tramways car No 11, built by Brush in 1907 and fitted with Mountain & Gibson radial truck and BTH electrical equipment, originally ran on the Dolter stud principle. It is pictured *c*1929 beside the Vaughan Parade offices of Timpson's and of Royal Blue — not W. E. Cawdle's home-grown Torquay version but that of Elliott Bros (Bournemouth) Ltd.
Colin Morris collection

Inside the Torquay Tramways car-shed at St Marychurch are (at the rear) one of the original three-bay double-deck cars and (in front) two four-bay single-deck cars, ex-Taunton Electric Traction Co Ltd in 1921. What look, at a glance, like upper-deck 'decency panels' are, in fact, advertisement boards around the roof. All Torquay's trams were built by Brush.
Colin Shears collection

subsidiary companies in the provinces. NEC's local example was the Torquay Tramways Co Ltd, which was destined to play a crucial part in the history of the future Devon General Omnibus & Touring Co Ltd.

The NEC installed as Manager and Engineer Mr H. Holliday. He arranged for the necessary electricity to be supplied by Torquay Corporation, which promptly extended its generating works accordingly. As had happened earlier in Bournemouth (see *Glory Days: Bournemouth Transport*) the decision-makers of Torquay saw that unsightly poles and overhead wires were inappropriate for their beautiful town. Whereas Bournemouth opted for the conduit-rail system (which filled with sand, horse manure and mud, causing its early

Clock Tower and Strand, Torquay

replacement by the 'unsightly' overhead), NEC chose for Torquay the Dolter system — electrified metal studs in cylinders buried between the rails and brought to the surface by a magnetised skate fixed beneath each tram as it passed along the track. This operation created spectacular flashes and sparks, together with crackling noises and a sulphurous smell — a combination of fire and brimstone magnified where and when salt water sprayed over the sea wall. The Corporation was finally convinced that the company's preferred overhead system should be substituted after an unfortunate cab horse trod on a stud which hadn't retracted — and was promptly electrocuted.

Torquay Tramways' first three routes — Beacon Quay–Torre station, Brunswick Square–Upton–St Marychurch and St Marychurch–Ellacombe–Union Street — began operation on 4 April 1907. They were followed in November of that year by another, from Strand to St Marychurch via Babbacombe. With the opening of the latter it became possible to operate a popular

circular tour during the summer months. The main depot was located off Westhill Avenue, St Marychurch, within cheering distance of Torquay Football Club's ground at Plainmoor. In 1908 the tracks were extended along Torbay Road to the Grand Hotel — the closest they came to Torquay station — and then further south to Paignton railway station, which section opened on 17 July 1911. A four-track car shed to support the latter was opened off Torquay Road, Preston. By the end of that year the whole system had been converted to overhead supply.

Like the rest of those in the West Country, all Torquay's double-deck trams were open-top. Cars Nos 1-18 worked initially upon the Dolter system. Cars 19-33, to the same three-bay pattern, were delivered in 1910 and commenced service on the Paignton line the following year. In 1921 three second-hand single-deck trams (Nos 34-6) were acquired from Taunton. Finally, between 1923 and 1925, six large four-bay bogie (eight-wheel) cars (Nos 37-42) offered 76 seats and an extremely

The Mallock Memorial Clock Tower looms large as Torquay Tramways car No 9 sets off past the cab-stand in the Strand on a Dolter-system track (see text), the studs being visible at intervals between the rails. An early occupier of the omnibus stand is the Torquay Road Car Co's Clarkson 17-seater steam bus (CA 150), ex-Vale of Llangollen and, earlier (as BP 319) the Sussex Motor Road Car Co Ltd. *Colin Morris collection*

13

One steam-bus operator which started up in July 1911 — long after the Torquay Tramways began running — was the Torquay–Chelston Steam Car Co Ltd, its first garage at the rear of 43/45 Market Street. This is that company's first vehicle, a 20-seat Clarkson IV (T 2086), which set off on routes which did not compete directly with the tramways company's cars. *Colin Morris collection*

Whilst all this stage-carriage activity was becoming established, so too were the foundations laid for the famous Grey Cars coaching business. Originally an operating arm of the South Devon Garage & Motor Touring Co, the 'Grey Torpedo Cars' started with just three cars. One of a pair of 24-seat Commer charabancs with chain drive, T 3994 entered service fifth, in November 1913. *Colin Morris collection*

comfortable ride. All 42 cars had been assembled by the Brush Electrical Engineering Co Ltd at the Falcon Works, Loughborough. The track gauge was the same as Exeter's (3ft 6in). The original fleetname displayed upon the cars was 'The Torquay Electric Tramways'; this was later changed to 'The Torquay Tramways Company Ltd' and thereafter variously 'Torquay Tramways Company Ltd' and 'The Torquay Tramways Co Ltd'. Fleet livery was maroon and cream, the latter becoming much yellower by the end of the 'Twenties.

This, then, was the established means of road passenger transport in Torquay and along the road to Paignton when, in 1919, the Devon General Omnibus & Touring Co Ltd arrived in the area and set out to establish a foothold there.

Throughout the lengthy period outlined here there was, as befitted an area of Devon bejewelled with attractive scenery, a growing trade in the tours and excursions sector. The latter — starting, of course, in the days of horse-drawn carriages and making a parallel transition to mechanical traction — remained largely in the hands of local operators for somewhat longer, in some cases remarkably so. This aspect of the Devon General story is covered briefly in Chapter 5.

2. Grist to the Mill — and French

In transport histories to date John Stuart Mill is credited with having 'founded Devon General in Exeter'. Like many things in life, it wasn't as simple as that. Indeed, if one takes 'founded' to mean endowed with sufficient funds to get such a business started, in Devon General's case the cash came from way beyond the bounds of Devon. It came instead from South East London, Littlehampton (Sussex) and, later, Margate (Kent) — and was placed initially in the safekeeping of the Catford branch of the London County & Westminster & Parr's Bank Ltd. More outsiders were about to acquire holdings put to good use in the county of Devon.

The Devon General Omnibus & Touring Co Ltd (Company No 155374) was registered at Companies House in London on 22 May 1919. The directors were: Charles Mill (Chairman), a commercial traveller of 2 Kilmorie Road, Forest Hill SE23 (300 shares), John Stuart Mill, an engineer and son of Charles (shares and £8 per week wages), Harry Clark, a retired ironmonger of Littlehampton, Thomas Timberley, a fruit-grower of Littlehampton (250 shares) and Ernest David Bullock, an accountant of London SE23 (100 shares). As later events would disclose, it was the last-named who orchestrated the setting up of the company.

The authorised initial capital of the firm was £4,000, of which £3,500 had been subscribed by the following September, and its registered office was located in the front room of Charles Mill's modest semi-detached house at the northern end of Kilmorie Road.

By June 1919 a No 2 account had been set up at Exeter, and Percy J. Grist had been appointed Secretary. Whether or not he was a relative of the Grist family long-established as carriage proprietors in Torquay I have not been able to discover, but it is conceivable that it was upon his suggestion that the location was chosen. John Stuart Mill, meanwhile, had been designated General Manager, his task to set up and run the company in Devon.

J. S. Mill had learned his trade as a motor engineer with Jarrott & Letts, of 45 Great Marlborough Street, Soho, the firm being concessionaires for Bugatti, Crossley and Lorraine de Dietrich cars before World War 1. There can be little doubt that his was the initial idea for setting up a bus company. With his contacts in the industry he would have known what was afoot at the close of the war in the London General/AEC works at Walthamstow, in particular the fitting of war-surplus AEC YC lorry chassis with retained B-type open-top bus bodywork 'plus a few bits' and of a stored collection of 180 AEC YC 27-seat lorry-buses released by the Ministry of Munitions, both types considered standard interim equipment at that time for the London General Omnibus Co Ltd and anyone else who could be persuaded to buy them. Having approached the local authorities in Devon as early as February 1919, Mill initially chose three of the former, transferring ownership of them to the new company upon its foundation in return for his shares. The substitution of 'Devon' for 'London' led to an obvious choice of name — and the LGOC livery was retained as well.

John Stuart Mill, son of the company's first Chairman, purchased three vehicles from the Walthamstow works of AEC and sold them to the new company in exchange for shares and the post of General Manager. It had been brought to his notice that there was a lack of passenger-transport facilities in South Devon, and there can be little doubt that the initial concept for a bus service in the area was his. *Colin Morris*

This modest semi-detached house in Forest Hill, South London, was the first registered office of the Devon General Omnibus & Touring Co Ltd. It was here, in the spring of 1919, that meetings hosted by occupier Charles Mill, his son John and an accountant, Ernest Bullock, led to the formal setting up of the company and its registration on 22 May 1919. The first few meetings of the board of directors were held there also. *Colin Morris*

J. S. Mill and Percy Grist travelled
down to Exeter and arranged to house
the vehicles at E. J. Hancock's Exeter
Garage Co premises in Paris Street from
1 July 1919, at a rental of £2 per week.
The first bus was ready a little early
and arrived on 28 June.

Soon afterwards Grist resigned his
briefly held post of Secretary to take up a
position which he felt was more agreeable
to him — a simple decision which was
later to have considerable ramifications.
As a result the board replaced Grist's
co-authorisation to draw upon the
company's imprest account at Exeter with
an authority requiring J. S. Mill's signature
alone. Although clearly a hard-working go-
getter, sadly, over the next 21 months, Mill
was to prove something of a loose cannon.
Said to be related to the much better-
known 19th-century author, economist,

philosopher, champion of women's
suffrage and Liberal MP for Westminster,
John Stuart Mill (and, indeed, named after
him), J. S. Mill the second seemed to have
inherited one of his forebear's few
weaknesses; in his extremely fine book
A Short History of Our Own Times (1885),
Justin McCarthy MP wrote of J. S. Mill MP
that 'he had given some offence in various
quarters by a too-great independence of
action and expression'. Much had been
achieved, however, before these chickens
came home to roost for Mill the Younger,
his father Charles and 200-share-holding
mother Mary Ann.

By September 1919 it was clear there
was sufficient traffic to add further vehicles
to the three working on two routes between
Exeter and Torquay — one via Chudleigh
and the other via Dawlish. It was decided
to purchase two saloon buses, two
charabancs and a couple of lorry-buses —
and to award James Wheeler £25 for
allowing his pub in Exeter to be used as
the first Devon General booking office.

In less than three months the original
trio of AECs had produced a net profit of
£1,097. Latterly a parcel service had been
introduced and was showing a steadily
increasing profit. Although Torquay
Tramways had already laid plans to set up
its own bus services in the area, it was felt,
rightly or not, that Devon County Council
had granted some kind of exclusive
running-rights over the routes presently
being worked by Devon General — and
any other which might be agreed upon
in the future.

Accordingly, as 1919 came to a close,
more funds were forthcoming from
Littlehampton. Harry Clark had been
rallying more support on the Sussex coast:
Mrs Elizabeth Mann, Harry Smart,
Dr Robert Goring, E. J. Mortimer

VON GENERAL OMNIBUS & TOURING COMPANY,
LIMITED.

Directors:

CHARLES MILL (Chairman),
JOHN STUART MILL (General Manager),
ERNEST D. BULLOCK (Accountant),
HARRY CLARK,
THOMAS TIMBERLEY.

Report of the Directors and Accounts
to 30th JUNE, 1920.

To be presented to the FIRST ANNUAL GENERAL MEETING to be held at the DARTMOUTH HOTEL, DARTMOUTH ROAD, FOREST HILL, LONDON, S.E. 23, at 2.30 p.m., on SATURDAY, the 28th AUGUST, 1920.

1. The Directors present the Accounts for the period ending 30th June, 1920.
2. The Total Receipts for Revenue Account amounted to £7,758 8 6
   and the Expenditure to £6,859 15 0½
   Leaving a Balance of £898 13 5½
   The appropriation of this balance will be discussed and decided upon at the General Meeting.
3. The operations of the Company are extending and more capital is necessary. The Directors, therefore, recommend that the Capital be increased.
4. All the Directors retire and offer themselves for re-election.
5. The retiring Auditors, Messrs. Brooks, Williams & Co., offer themselves for re-election.

By Order of the Board,
CHARLES MILL,
Chairman.

20th August, 1920.

The new company's enthusiasm for double-deckers waned rapidly when it discovered just how much tree-lopping was involved, whereafter a decision was taken to purchase only single-deck vehicles. Thus AECs 4 and 5 (T 7750/2) were fitted with saloon bodywork by Hora. The latter pauses at Woodbury *en route* to Budleigh Salterton. Registration numbers with a solitary T (Devon) were issued alternately, odd numbers being allocated to motor cycles.
Calton Phoenix

AEC YCs 6 and 7 were fitted with 28-seat charabanc bodywork built locally by A. G. Dowell, of Russell Street, Exeter. It was said that AEC was so satisfied with the workmanship that it placed a contract with Dowell's for similar bodies to be sent to other operators. One of the pair stands outside the offices of the Mutual Life Insurance Co Ltd at Bedford Circus, Exeter, as the knock-kneed and bow-legged stand guard.
Calton Phoenix

Some 180 AEC YC lorries released by the Ministry of Munitions after World War 1 were made available for use by the London General Omnibus Co Ltd as emergency buses. A staircase attached to the rear gave access to 25 of the 27 seats. Mill acquired two such vehicles, which became Nos 8 and 9 (T 8232/4) in the Devon General fleet. This side elevation gives an idea of what they looked like. *Colin Morris*

When not in use for passengers the AEC lorry-buses doubled as goods and parcel-delivery vehicles. Also dedicated largely to that task was an American-built Federal 25hp, 2-ton canvas-hooded lorry. Leslie Folkard has recorded this vehicle (T 9234) in use also as a charabanc, in which guise it may have carried the fleet number 10. Mill's transaction with Whiting Ltd for this chassis did not have board approval. *Colin Morris*

and Arthur Robinson were among those recruited to the cause, whilst Thomas Timberley doubled his shareholding.

Hora-bodied AEC YC saloon buses Nos 4 and 5 were ready for delivery in January 1920, and an Exeter coachbuilder had been commissioned to provide charabanc bodies for two further YC chassis in time for the summer season. In April Charles Mill and Ernest Bullock visited a site in Exeter and another in Newton Abbot thought suitable for the erection of garages. Plans for the latter fell through, but the Exeter site — in Blackboy Road — was purchased from the Exeter Co-operative & Industrial Society Ltd for £2,300. This was to prove the acquisition which enabled Devon General to take firm root in the county. That summer the company also began negotiating for a site in Exmouth. The nominal capital, raised to £15,000 in September 1919, was increased to £20,000 in August 1920.

In the autumn of 1920 a garage site, shop and house were indeed purchased in Exeter Road, Exmouth. J. S. Mill promptly moved into that house, at a rental of £26 per annum. A similar site, also incorporating a shop and a house, was earmarked for purchase at Kingsteignton (rather than Newton Abbot), and J. S. Mill personally accepted the tender of £1,491 10s 0d from Messrs Stock & Collings to undertake the provision of the ironwork for the garage to be built there.

The year 1920 ended, however, with the first sign of a rift among the directors. W. J. Holmes, a retired publican of Margate and by now the largest shareholder in the company, was considered ready to join the board. Clearly Charles Mill, his friend, wished him to be appointed Secretary. Unfortunately, this item on the agenda of the meeting, held — ironically — at the Dartmouth Hotel, Forest Hill, London, was listed at No 2, whereas the appointment of a new director was No 3. After a prickly moment when Charles Mill dissented and temporarily quit the chair, Ernest Bullock the accountant was also elected Secretary — and W. J. Holmes became merely a director.

More importantly, from an historical point of view in particular, an equitable mortgage upon the properties at Exeter and Exmouth was granted to Barclays Bank, Exeter, to secure an overdraft of £5,000. And at the same meeting, on 4 December 1920, the board discussed negotiations with 'a Mr French' — and Bullock was instructed to prepare a balance sheet for him. The company was in financial trouble, and that already famous 'mover and shaker' of the early motor-bus industry, Walter Flexman

French, of Balham (see *Glory Days: Maidstone & District*), was to be called in to straighten things out.

By February 1921, there having been no response to an appeal for further capital to meet the cost of the garages now under construction, Guests Trust Ltd offered to finance and take control of the company. This the directors considered, along with an option to wind up the company there and then. Instead, it was decided to convert it into a public company by extending the list of shareholders.

The feathers finally flew for the Mill family at a meeting in the Dartmouth Hotel on 4 April 1921. The 'conduct of the company's business at Exeter by Mr J. S. Mill' was laid before the directors by Bullock. The details are not listed in the minutes, but it would appear that much had been done which the directors found themselves simply 'approving', rather than 'instructing' (as was their right) that this or that should be undertaken on their behalf. That J. S. Mill, as the 'late manager', was afterward sent the bill

Initially called in to steady the ship, Walter Flexman French — one of the leading pioneers of the industry — found himself instead offered the chairmanship of the company. This he accepted. He promptly moved the registered office to the Blackboy Road garage, Exeter, substituted new Articles of Association and sought additional funds.
But it was a case of too little, too late: the Torquay Tramways Co was in sight of success.
Colin Morris collection

The company's headed notepaper now bears the name of Ernest Bullock as General Manager and Secretary. A 'to whom it may concern' notice for Inspector Tucker, it was signed by Max Colyer Fergusson, a subscriber to the firm. A two-stroke motorcycle ridden by the inspector was bought by Devon General from Tucker himself, for 12 monthly instalments of £30 added to his wages — not the sign of a company in funds.
Philip Platt collection

Extent of Devon General routes, 1921.

Exterior of the company's main garage and head office at Blackboy Road, Exeter.
Colin Morris collection

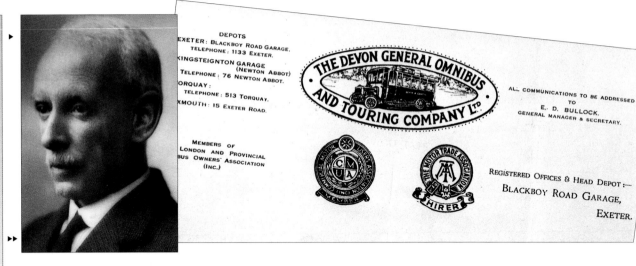

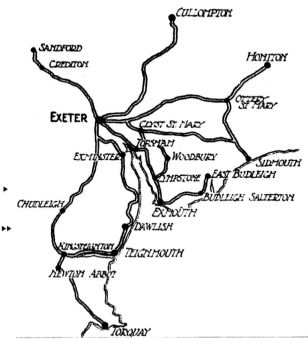

for 'the Humber and Federal [vehicle] transactions' gives a clue as to what may have displeased them.

Whatever, Charles Mill and J. S. Mill resigned their positions with the company forthwith, and, temporarily at least, Ernest Bullock's star shone — so much so that, when thereafter he was interviewed for an article eventually published by *Motor Transport* in January 1922, the correspondent was informed that the Devon General Omnibus & Transport Co Ltd 'was formed by Mr Bullock himself in May 1919'. Whether or not James Stuart Mill, in his over-enthusiastic efforts to launch the company, quite deserved that, is a moot point.

Thomas Timberley promptly became Chairman *pro tem*, because negotiations with Walter Flexman French and his colleague Max Colyer Fergusson were already well underway. Was there,

to quote a pithy phrase from a lady of *our* own time (with a solid Devonshire name), 'something of the night' about all this?

Ernest Bullock moved house and home to Exeter, taking up residence at 7 Haven Road, and, with effect from 2 May 1921, became General Manager and Secretary of the company. Walter Flexman French subscribed for 1,000 shares and became Chairman. Max Colyer Fergusson agreed to take up 3,000 shares and was appointed Traffic Manager. E. J. Mortimer — he of Littlehampton — agreed to apply for 3,000 also, and became manager of the Kingsteignton garage, at a salary of £400 per annum. A future role as directors was contemplated for both Fergusson and Mortimer. The latter took as his local base the

house attached to the garage at Kingsteignton, whilst French engaged as the company's engineer H. G. Shute, who was to last only until the end of that year of 1921.

Walter Flexman French now substituted his more-or-less standard Articles of Association for the company (for an outline see *Glory Days: Maidstone & District*, page 8), moved the company's registered office from Forest Hill to the almost complete Blackboy Road garage in Exeter and began a process of converting the fleet into one comprised solely of single-deckers. Three additional AEC YC saloons (chassis Nos 8872, 9607 and 11588) were purchased, for £3,939, and fitted with Dodson CD19 34-seat bodies; six Daimler Y chassis were ordered from

21

Capt Headley at the Slough Trading Co, three charabanc bodies being obtained from the same source and two saloon bodies (for £85 each) from the East Kent Road Car Co Ltd (the chassis being sent to Canterbury for fitment), French also sounding out other companies for a further saloon body.

Meanwhile, at both Exeter and Kingsteignton, a small amount of private-car repairs and the supply of petrol and oil to the public was undertaken; and, in a typical piece of W. F. French diversification, on 1 October 1921 the company signed a one-year contract to run a Hallford van for biscuit-makers Macfarlane, Lang & Co Ltd and carry out that firm's deliveries within a radius of 60 miles from Exeter.

Devon General was still feeling the pinch, however, particularly from the competition of the rival bus operations of the Torquay Tramways Co, whose motor-bus fleet now outnumbered its own (following the entry into service with TTC of six AEC K-type double-deckers) and, to a lesser extent, those of the Devon Motor Transport Co Ltd and the Sidmouth Motor Co Ltd. E. J. Mortimer and Torquay Tramways' Henry Nesbitt engaged in preliminary discussions locally which led to a series of talks in London between French and William Cownie, Managing Director of the

National Electric Construction Co Ltd (Torquay Tramways' holding company), while French also engaged in peace-making correspondence with Maj W. P. Colfox, father-in-law of the proprietor of DMT.

All this coincided with an opportunity which came and evaporated in short order during the winter of 1921/2 — the offer by Exeter City Council to discuss with Devon General the purchase or lease by the company of Exeter City Tramways' complete operation. While discussions with the Council were ongoing Torquay Tramways stunned Devon General by obtaining for its motor buses the lease of a garage at Arthur Kirby's Saw Mills in The Avenue, Newton Abbot — a town where Devon General had tried unsuccessfully to establish itself from the outset.

Meanwhile, services had been extended by Bullock and French beyond the territory established by Mill — to Crediton and Sandford, to Cullompton, to Ottery St Mary and Honiton, to Sidmouth and to East Budleigh. It seems likely, however, that the steam had gone out of French's efforts to expand in Devon, for his 'greater plan' had already gone awry. The clue lies with the recent breaking-off of takeover talks with Butler Bros (Bridport) Ltd for the acquisition of its Bridport–Lyme Regis–Axminster service. French was at the time Chairman also of Hants & Dorset Motor Services Ltd — and of Southdown and Maidstone & District. He had wished for 'his' Hants & Dorset to run westward to Bridport, Lyme Regis or Charmouth to link up with 'his' Devon General. In the event Thomas Attree's Road Motors Ltd of Luton had turned up at Weymouth in late 1921, putting a wedge into the centre of that plan. Thus French had missed by a whisker being able to claim that it would be possible to travel in 'his' service buses all the way from Buckfastleigh to Faversham in Kent.

Possibly now half-heartedly looking to secure Devon General's eastern flank, in the face of some additional competition emanating from Tiverton, in the form of a new operator, Croscols Ltd, French now sought for an agreement with the National Omnibus & Transport Co Ltd (not associated in any shape or form with the National Electric Construction Co Ltd — or the much later National Bus Company), whose linear march westward across Southern England had become a cause for much concern at Devon General.

The initiative, however, was taken by this 'other' National company. In March 1922 NO&T asked for 3,000 shares in Devon General. French, one of the original 'boundary-fixers' in Southern England (c1911) held out until, on 8 May 1922, he had to hand an agreement signed by National's Secretary and Transport Manager, Bert Smith. It was a boundary agreement — for 10 years and renewable by consent, whereby: (a) the road from Minehead to Sidmouth via Bampton, Tiverton, Cullompton, Honiton and Ottery St Mary was in the Devon General Omnibus & Touring Co's area, (b) the road from Honiton to Axminster was to be operated by Devon General, and (c) the road from Axminster to Charmouth was to be a joint operation, Devon General and National Omnibus & Transport. At this stage, at least, National had agreed not to operate west of line (a).

This was considered good enough. National received shares Nos 28636-31635 and, at a meeting held in Upper Richmond Road, Putney, on 25 May 1922, National's Walter James Iden was appointed a director of Devon General. Oh, how close National came to obtaining the foothold which took its successor Western National nearly half a century to achieve completely. Both the National holding and Iden's directorship of Devon General were to last exactly . . . one month! For, at that same meeting, the last item on the agenda was an offer from Torquay Tramways Ltd to purchase all the shares of Devon General. Iden must have been somewhat deflated to hear the board leave that matter in the hands of Walter Flexman French 'to make the best terms possible for the sale of the business'.

The last meeting of the independent Devon General Omnibus & Touring Co Ltd was held in the office of French's solicitor, Stuart Green, at 22 Southampton Street, Holborn, London. Present were directors French, Iden, Clark, Timberley, Holmes and Bullock, with Mortimer and Fergusson attending to secure recompense for loss of office. NEC was not directly involved in the meeting, save that 'interim directors' Cyril Tuson and Lewis

Jacobs were appointed to represent Torquay Tramways in the presence of NEC's solicitor and auditor.

The capital of Devon General at that time stood at £40,000 in £1 shares, with 31,635 issued as fully paid. The purchase price paid in the name of the Torquay Tramways Co Ltd was £36,000 for the undertaking and assets, free from liability, save a mortgage of £10,000 taken out by the retiring directors the previous month upon the premises at Exeter, Exmouth and Kingsteignton, for which the purchasers indemnified them against all liabilities.

The major assets to be acquired by Torquay Tramways were the freehold garages at Blackboy Road, Exeter, and 15 Exeter Road, Exmouth, the leasehold one at Newton Abbot Road, Kingsteignton, 19 single-deck passenger-service vehicles, the Federal lorry and a Humber parcel van. The contracts to be taken over included: advertising upon tickets, the training of three

As its rival faltered the Torquay Tramways bus operation went from strength to strength. It concluded its 1922 purchasing programme by adding nine 32-seat Strachan & Brown-bodied saloons, eight of them based on Daimler Y chassis. The exception was a 1920 AEC YC — the remains of a vehicle destroyed by fire at St Marychurch on 3 June 1921. The new combination retained the chassis' original fleet number (3).
Colin Morris collection

AEC YC No 3 (now TA 3094 in lieu of the original T 8192) carried the specimen Strachan & Brown body featured in the trade press at the time. The seemingly austere interior was described as extremely comfortable, with roomy seats which were deep and 'built on springs'. When all the windows were dropped the body was fully open. A semi-isolated smoking compartment was provided at the rear.
Colin Morris collection

Back at struggling Devon General the fleet continued to grow slowly to its peak — during the company's independent existence — of 19 vehicles. Nos 14-16 (FJ 1697-9) were AEC YCs; fitted with Dodson CD19 bodywork, the chassis were on hire-purchase from AEC. Much of their work was done on the Exeter–Newton Abbot–Torquay route. In front of No 15 is Inspector Walter H. Tucker on his P&S motorcycle.
Philip Platt collection

On 26 June 1922 came the now inevitable. All the shares of the Devon General Omnibus & Touring Co Ltd were transferred to Torquay Tramways Co Ltd, whose nominees replaced the board and officers of the independent company.
This would lead to the formation of a combined fleet — and scenes such as this: ex-Torquay Tramways Co vehicles garaged as far east as the Mill Street garage at Sidmouth.
Philip Platt collection

▲ An additional brake upon whatever expansion plans Devon General managed to retain in hope, rather than expectation, was the continued presence of the Great Western Railway's Road Motor Department and its activities in the area around Paignton and Totnes. Pictured at Kingsbridge, GWR No 228 (T 8148) was a 1920-vintage AEC YC with GWR in-house bodywork. *Ian Allan Library*

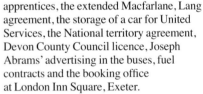

apprentices, the extended Macfarlane, Lang agreement, the storage of a car for United Services, the National territory agreement, Devon County Council licence, Joseph Abrams' advertising in the buses, fuel contracts and the booking office at London Inn Square, Exeter.

The retiring directors of the previously independent Devon General were precluded for five years from participating in any way in bus or charabanc business west of the line Minehead to Sidmouth or east of the line Bideford to Plymouth. This territorial statement of intent by Torquay Tramways — for that is what it amounted to — would have raised eyebrows at the Hardy Central Garage in Minehead and at Colwills (Ilfracombe) Ltd but would prove a viable way out of their difficulties for the three directors of the 'intruding' Croscols Ltd of Tiverton, less than three years later.

3. NEC's Devon General

The National Electric Construction Co Ltd had been founded in 1897 as the National Electric Free Wiring Co Ltd. Presumably because too many wags had asked for their gift of free copper wire, two years later the word 'Free' was dropped from its title — it had only meant 'we wire your house for free — and charge only for what you use'. The firm had become NEC in 1903. Its portfolio of subsidiary companies eventually included the Mexborough & Swinton Traction Co Ltd, the City of Oxford Motor Services Ltd, South Wales Commercial Motors Ltd, the Rhondda Tramways Co Ltd and, of course, Torquay Tramways Co Ltd. That portfolio now included the Devon General Omnibus & Touring Co Ltd — as a *pro tem* subsidiary of its Torquay Tramways subsidiary — whose registered office now went back to London, at NEC's HQ at 62/63 Queen Street, EC4.

In early August 1922 Daniel Campbell, previously Traffic Superintendent of the City of Oxford company, joined Devon General to direct its operations from Exeter, whilst Henry J. Nisbett of Torquay Tramways remained as Engineer and Manager at Torquay. A house for Campbell to rent was purchased at 1 Morley Road, Exeter.

Later that month, their work done, Tuson and Jacobs withdrew, and Harold Barnett was elected Chairman of Devon General. He was destined to hold that post for 20 years (plus a further four as a director) — the longest chairmanship in the company's history. Among those elected to directorships in the company, Barnett comes closest to being 'proper Devon', having been educated at the Kings School, Ottery St Mary. His initial fellow directors were Benjamin Stedham, Arthur Radford, Henry

J. Nesbitt and William Brodie Cownie, Managing Director of NEC.

On 28 August 1922 and in fulfilment of one of those 'in house' readjustments of capital and resources carried out by related subsidiaries, NEC's 'new boys' DGO&T 'acquired' the omnibus undertaking of the Torquay Tramways Co Ltd — which by that stage was twice the size of its own. At the time the DGO&T capital was £110,000, of which 21,635 preference shares, fully paid up, were held by the Tramways company.

In return for the 'acquisition' of its bus and charabanc business Torquay Tramways was to receive a further 65,365 shares, comprising £48,486 for goods and chattels, £11,587 for the grant of a 60-year lease of the garage, workshops and buildings on a 2,000sq yd plot adjacent to its St Marychurch tramway depot (at a rate of £20 per annum, with option to buy the freehold for £200), £4,337 for goodwill and £955 for other assets 'not capable of manual delivery'. Among the goods and chattels DGO&T thus acquired an additional 23 omnibuses and 13 charabancs. And the identity of this new and newly enlarged Devon General Omnibus & Touring Co Ltd remained intact, as Company No 155374.

This accomplished, William Cownie became Managing Director of Devon General and, together with his newly appointed General Manager, Daniel Campbell, went forward into the next decade with considerable vigour — and set the enlarged company firmly upon its feet. Cownie, an impressive figure in any scenario, had played rugby in the purple and white hoops of Watson's Academy, Edinburgh, for Scotland in a turn-of-the-century team which twice beat England and for London Scottish

◄ William Brodie Cownie, Managing Director of Devon General 1922-32, appointed by the National Electric Construction Co Ltd to oversee the affairs of yet another of its subsidiaries. A mixture of Scottish grit, determination and a sense of direction, plus NEC funds to back it, was now brought to bear. An ex-Scottish international rugby player, Cownie was a big man in every sense of the word. *Colin Morris*

◄ Daniel Campbell, General Manager of Devon General 1922-33. Although he was a football fanatic, Campbell 'plus Cownie' proved to be the winning team which turned around the fortunes of the company. Perhaps because he too had a good Scottish pedigree, Campbell and his Managing Director saw eye to eye on most things and became firm friends — to the great good of Devon General. *Colin Morris*

Whilst the expansionist policy of the new NEC-controlled Devon General was put in train the former Torquay Tramways motor buses were given 'Devon General' fleetnames and legal-address blocks, while a darker-than-London General red was now the norm. Initially the original Tramways fleet numbers took precedence: No 1 (T 8188) was photographed in Cullompton.
The Omnibus Society

'Croscols' was set up at Tiverton — with an initial push from Crosville at Chester (see text) — in December 1920. Two Daimler CKs (FM 1941/2), driven down from Chester by fitters Chowne and Sweet respectively, arrived in the winter of 1920/1. Looking elegant and sporting a cane (at centre) is Capt Harold Youlton, the prime mover. The firm's vehicles and goodwill were destined to be acquired by Devon General in March 1924. *Calton Phoenix*

until, at the age of 22, he gave up the game to concentrate upon his work with NEC.

In contrast, Daniel Campbell was an Association football fanatic, and it was said that many employees of Devon General under his managership had been engaged on the basis of how well they could play the game. The 'Cownie Cup' was established, and the Devon General team played regularly on a knock-out basis against other representative teams from the NEC group.

The restructured company added two small-capacity Daimler CB saloons to the fleet, following the example of Croscols, and in October 1923 fitted one of them with 'giant pneumatic tyres' as an experiment. On 21 March 1924 the vehicles, stock in trade and goodwill of Croscols Ltd of Tiverton was purchased for £2,250 — of which only £10 was for the goodwill.

Croscols Ltd (Company No 175591) had been incorporated on 7 July 1921 with a nominal capital of £10,000. Although Claude Crosland Taylor, of the Crosville Motor Co Ltd (not 'Services' until 1929), Chester, was clearly involved, no structural or financial evidence exists that Croscols was 'a subsidiary of

Colwills (Ilfracombe) Ltd' (as has been suggested elsewhere), set up openly by Crosland Taylor in February 1920 with two local directors and considerable financial backing from subscribers based on the Wirral in Cheshire and from the Crosville Motor Co Ltd in particular. In the case of Croscols Ltd the first and last four letters were clearly intended to support such a notion, but, paradoxically, none of the directors or subscribers was the same. The Colwills (Ilfracombe) Ltd set-up belongs in another book, but Croscols' structural origins were as follows: Capt Harold Leslie Youlton possibly met Crosland Taylor in Chester. He is not listed as a private resident of that area, but he may have been based there with Western Command during the World War 1 wind-down. On the other hand his father, Harry Joseph Youlton, of Penarth, Glamorgan, a subscriber to Croscols (together with nine major shareholders from the South Wales shipping industry), was a 'paint manufacturer'. So too was the 'odd man out' geographically in

this category, Arthur J. Davis, of Rock Ferry, Wirral, Cheshire. And he is believed to have been the supplier to the Crosland Taylor family of the beautiful dove-grey paint which was the original overall livery of Crosville, Colwills (Ilfracombe) Ltd and at least the first two Daimlers sent down to Tiverton from Chester in the winter of 1920/1. Perhaps it was Davis who introduced Capt Youlton to Claude Crosland Taylor as being able and available. It is noteworthy that Crosville enthusiasts of long-standing have not heard of Youlton, nor of the Taylors' Devon connections — not surprising, because there's not a whisper

The Brush-bodied AEC Y-type double-deckers — this one based at Newton Abbot — were given the revised Devon General livery . . .

. . . as was No 36 (TA 3800), a Daimler Y saloon, photographed at The Lawn, Sidmouth, on 27 March 1925, in the care of Driver Rendell of Sidmouth depot (centre). *Calton Phoenix (both)*

Samuel Garland joined Croscols in January 1921. This was his cap badge, probably the last to survive. Samuel Garland joined Devon General and drove until his retirement.
Calton Phoenix / Colin Morris

Capt Youlton added a locally registered Daimler Y charabanc and followed that by 'selling' Croscols to a new company, 'Croscols Ltd', incorporated on 7 July 1921. Two Daimler CB 20-seaters (TA 4851, 5391) followed, with bodywork supplied by Roberts of Shepherd's Bush. One of these is seen parked outside Hamlin's corn shop: Croscols' registered office was located behind the left-hand upstairs window.
Calton Phoenix

Apart from a market-day service from Tiverton to Bampton and Dulverton (on Tuesdays) Croscols' main territorial thrust was to the south — into Devon General's operating area, or on routes upon which the latter had its sights. Such competition made a takeover inevitable. Further information about Croscols and its activities may be obtained by contacting Roger Grimley (see Bibliography).
Roger Grimley collection

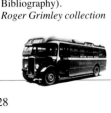

about them in the official Crosville records. However, the first Eaton-bodied Daimler saloon bus arrived at Tiverton in December 1920, to be joined by a sister vehicle the following month, and Youlton himself, turned up to sound out local traffic potential armed with a collection of Crosville tickets which were issued to his customers.

Before the official launch of Croscols Ltd Youlton acquired a locally registered Daimler Y charabanc, and all three vehicles were lodged initially at the Lamb Inn on the (later) A38 trunk road near Burlescombe. Perhaps that's where Youlton himself holed up at the start. At the formation proper of Croscols Ltd the official line reported Youlton as 'having agreed to sell his [*sic*] three motor vehicles, which are of the very latest type and practically new, at their cost price: two for £1,595 each and the third for £756, and transfer the goodwill of his business without charge . . .'.

There were at first just two directors; Charles Home Cecil Smith, of Villa Franca, Tiverton, and manager of the local textile factory of John Heathcoat & Co Ltd, and Youlton, now of Lowman View, Tiverton. Until the appointment of Edwin Munday as Secretary, Youlton himself carried out that task from an upstairs room above the local corn stores at 8 Fore Street. It must have smelled rather nice, but that's where the official headquarters of Croscols Ltd remained. On 23 April 1922 a third director, Frank Gregory Eastmond, a draper and coach operator of Daymond's Hill, Tiverton, was appointed. He owned two vehicles and a warehouse in Chapel Street; the latter became Croscols' garage, and his buses joined the fleet.

In an interview with Robert J. Crawley in July 1971 Samuel Garland, who had joined Youlton's staff in January 1921, recalled that other vehicles acquired were: Nos 5 and 6, second-hand Daimler CB type with Roberts-supplied bodywork, No 7, a 28-seat Daimler Y charabanc acquired from the Southampton area, No 8, a Daimler bus with rear entrance and longitudinal seating, the bodywork again supplied by Roberts — and 'a rather tatty LeRoi parcels van'. Interestingly the names of practically everyone who worked for Croscols, several of them employee shareholders, will remain on record at the West Country Historic Omnibus & Transport Trust, together with a list of the eight services operated, journey times and fares charged.

Rather than go too far north of Tiverton, as originally planned, Croscols had struck out for the South Coast, at Budleigh Salterton — very much into Devon General territory — and an additional bus was hired from Hardy's Garage of Minehead to help out with the traffic. That set the alarm bells ringing as to what the Hardy Central Garage Co Ltd was up to, and Devon General began to negotiate a boundary agreement with that firm. Yet, with the shares of Croscols called up at 6,400, in September 1923 Youlton was replaced as a director by his father, Harry. A local appointee, Jack Clutterbuck took up the management of the company, and Munday returned to his former post at the Heathcoat factory.

The following winter Claude Crosland Taylor decided to pull out of Devon as being 'too far away to control', according to a note scribbled on the back of a postcard many years later by his brother, Jim. This is the nearest thing we have to an admission that the Taylor family were ever involved in the passenger transport of the county. The paradox of the choice of name 'Croscols' therefore remains a mystery.

Hence Devon General made its acquisition of Croscols Ltd in March 1924, and for the following five years C. H. C. Smith was a director of DGO&T. At about the time of this purchase eight reconditioned Daimler Y chassis, at £255 each, were obtained from the Slough trade centre, together with four 40-seater Strachan & Brown bodies with anti-vibration springing devices at £510 each; plus one 'dual body' built by Thompson of Louth,

Built by Thompson & Co (Coach Builders) Ltd of Louth, Lincolnshire, and sold to Devon General for £400 was this dual-purpose body, which the operator had mounted upon a Daimler Y chassis. If the part painted cream were lifted off, the 'bus' became a 'charabanc' for summer use — all rather more complicated and space-consuming than was worthwhile. *Ian Allan Library*

New vehicles added to the fleet included a batch of four 32-seat Daimler Y saloons to help out with the new services acquired (and adapted) from Croscols and radiating from Tiverton. No 35 (TT 193) awaits its departure time thence to Exeter, with a passenger's 'go-kart' stacked alarmingly between wing and bonnet. *Calton Phoenix*

Among larger omnibus companies Devon General got into its stride with pneumatic tyres relatively early. In an amazingly coincidental pairing at Newton Abbot in the late 1920s the first-ever vehicle in the Devon General fleet (T 6942), which (unless this is an instance of a reissued registration) seems to have acquired a Daimler radiator and is now a charabanc, poses in the company of Torquay Tramways' last charabanc (TA 3848). *Alan Lambert collection*

Lincolnshire, for £400, to serve as a coach in summer and a saloon bus in winter.

In June 1924 an agreement with the Devon Motor Transport Co Ltd defined the area of running for that firm and DGO&T. DMT had previously competed upon the Exeter–Honiton route and then on the Exeter–Colyton road but now — from Monday 9 June 1924 — withdrew its services from Exeter to Okehampton and to Moretonhampstead in favour of Devon General. Simultaneously the Hardy Central Garage Co Ltd, which was about to complete its acquisition of that other 'Crosville inspired' company, Colwills (Ilfracombe) Ltd, agreed to an area-dividing line with DGO&T starting at Okehampton and going through Lapford, Witheridge to Bampton — and extending optimistically eastward to Wellington, in Somerset, the arrangement to last for 10 years from 8 July 1924. This gave Devon General a six-mile cushion to the north of Tiverton.

That autumn Devon General made a considerable move into the coaching business (see Chapter 5) and followed that by ordering, rather modestly, 'two small charabus bodies' from Thompson's of Louth at £390 each, to be fitted, presumably, to the two ex-Croscols Daimler CBs, which, recalled Samuel Garland, had their chassis specially extended by 6ft apiece for such a purpose. It also began to press for licences to operate a stage-carriage service over the Torbay Road route, seeking ideally to place a dozen of the latest buses on the Torquay–Paignton road.

It was granted eight — and found itself in a fares war with Ashcroft's Motors Ltd, also granted licences to run on the route. An agreement between the two was signed in June 1928.

Cownie himself travelled to Torquay to negotiate — on 3 January 1927 — for the purchase of the two Leyland saloon buses, tyres and accessories of the Torquay–Chelston Car Co Ltd, for £2,500. Oddly, this updated name (from 'Steam Car') was not registered at Companies House until November 1935 — and Ethel Williams, by now sadly the widow of its last Managing Director, saw to it that the Torquay–Chelston wasn't officially wound up until 13 October 1942.

Pressure was now brought to bear upon Ernest and Audrey Babington of Ashburton, who were running services to Newton Abbot and elsewhere. Indeed, Devon General set about acquiring premises in their home town — eventually used as a parcel office and waiting room, with accommodation for an inspector above. On 20 May 1927 DGO&T purchased the Babingtons' 11 vehicles and the goodwill of the passenger service work for £5,000, leaving them to carry on with a motor-car business at Ashburton.

After trying out the latest product of Dennis, in 1926 the company had ordered 10 ADC 506 saloons with 32-seat Hall Lewis bodywork. It was sufficiently pleased with them to order a further eight in 1927, for a bargain £1,000 each plus eight old Daimler Y vehicles taken in part exchange. However, 1928 saw a move away from the products of ADC, AEC and Daimler, and Leyland became the preferred chassis manufacturer. The move began with the ordering of eight Lion PLSC3 chassis fitted with 32-seat bodywork by the now favourite bodybuilder, Hall Lewis.

An interesting aspect of the purchase of Gullick's 'White Heather' touring business in April 1928 (see Chapter 5) is that the two Lancia charabancs involved passed into the Devon General fleet proper (probably Nos 108/9, sold in 1933) rather than joining Fleetcars; moreover it seems that there were others occupying the 1xx range of fleet numbers. The year closed with

the placing of an order of some significance — four Leyland Titan TD1 chassis, at £1,073 15s 6d each, to receive double-deck bodywork, by Hall Lewis, for delivery the following year — and the purchase (for £225) of land at Woolbrook, Sidmouth, for the erection of a garage. The contract for putting up the steelwork (£609) went to Walker Bros Ltd of Walsall, while the local firm of G. A. Northcote undertook the building work for £1,900. The company moved in (from its earlier premises in Mill Street) during 1930.

In September 1929 the board was informed that it had become necessary to make adjustments to the company's northern and western boundaries in order to gain a secure participation in a through access to Plymouth. In that city, the largest by far in Devon, Devon General was to retain 50% of the fares paid by local passengers within the city — and the right to refuse to pick up such passengers on outward buses if deemed appropriate (by the look of them, presumably). The notional western boundary for Devon General operations — that running north to south and vaguely described as 'a line drawn between Bude and Plymouth' — had been somewhat over-generous when it was hinted at in 1922, while the 1924 agreement with Hardy-Colwills had been equally unclear about what was to happen to the south of Okehampton. Now it became clear: Devon General's territory in the south and west would be confined to the north bank of the River Dart from its estuary to Totnes, the boundary running thence along the road to Buckfastleigh and north-west across Dartmoor to Okehampton. The South Hams peninsula was the newly

In October 1921 what was originally AEC YC lorry-bus No 9 (T 8234) received an ex-East Kent saloon body. That in turn was replaced by this unidentified bodywork upon the change to pneumatics in the mid-1920s. The bus was photographed at Sidbury in the care of Driver Shirwell, who (so Robert Crawley understands) married the young lady — which seems just as well! *Calton Phoenix*

In January 1927 Devon General purchased two Leyland saloon buses from the Torquay–Chelston Car Co Ltd (previously a steam-bus operator). The first, which became No 98 in the Devon General fleet, was a Leyland G7, photographed in the days before it received pneumatic tyres. The second, No 99, was a Leyland Lion PLSC1. *Colin Morris collection*

Devon General purchased the business of E. O. Babington of Ashburton in May 1927, after a degree of pressure was brought to bear. The sale included a freehold house and garage and a total of 11 vehicles, only three of which saw use with the company. This Lancia saloon had been employed upon Babington's service to Torquay. *Colin Morris collection*

31

First of the 'moderns' were six Leyland Lioness PLC1 saloons with coach-seated accommodation for 26 passengers, built by Hall Lewis for use on limited-stop services. Since 1922 a good relationship had existed between Daniel Campbell and Bert Smith of National, leading to some running 'beyond the fringes', which now tended to blur the distinction between stage-carriage and tour. *Colin Shears collection*

The last Devon General buses built on a high chassis frame, useful for lorries and the battlefield, were Leyland Lion PLSC3 models, delivered in 1928/9. Somewhat upstaged by Daniel Campbell's approved plan to modernise the fleet, they were all withdrawn in 1934. Here Hall Lewis-bodied No 115 (UO 7470) enjoys a little glory on a limited-stop service, in the care of Harry Luscombe. *Calton Phoenix*

At the start of the temporary marriage between AEC and Daimler, which created the Associated Daimler Company, Devon General took delivery of 18 ADC 505 models with 32-seat Hall Lewis bodywork. The special radiators created for ADC had not yet become available, so Devon General's examples had the AEC type. Hall Lewis was to become Devon General's chosen coachbuilder. *Philip Platt collection*

DEVON GENERAL OMNIBUS & TOURING COMPANY, LTD.

The words 'Devon General' are synonymous with efficiency

TRAVEL BY THE ALL RED CARS

Motor Bus & Char-a-banc Service Guide throughout South & East Devon

Embracing Sea, Hill, Dale, River and Moorland Scenery

ALL SERVICES START FROM

THE STRAND, TORQUAY

One of our modern Saloon Coaches, as used on Public Service, with adjustable windows and electrically lit throughout. The last word in comfort.

The first of what was, at the time, known as the 'modern' generation of vehicles came to Devon General in 1929 with the delivery of six Leyland Tiger TS2 coaches with Hall Lewis bodywork, distinguishable from later examples by the chevron-shaped louvres above the windows. In its later years No 132 (UO 9759) prepares to depart from Sidmouth on stage-carriage service 46 to Lyme Regis. *The Omnibus Society*

Following the departure to London of the AEC K-type open-toppers in 1926 Devon General was for the second — and last — time an operator solely of single-deck vehicles. That was remedied in 1929 with the purchase of four Leyland Titan TD1s with Hall Lewis bodies. The variations in style and separated delivery dates suggest a trial batch. No 138 (DV 225), photographed in Exeter, was a highbridge model.
Mallory Saltmarsh collection

Probably all three of Leyland Titans 139-41 (DV 2149, 2304, 2356) were of lowbridge configuration; certainly this applies to the bus illustrated here and to that in the following picture. The reduced height is evident at cantrail level and in the between-decks panelling. They seem to have introduced the comparatively short-lived 'black band' livery of this period.
Mallory Saltmarsh collection

This offside view of a lowbridge Leyland Titan TD1 helps demonstrate the detail and livery variations in the batch — the number of bays, louvres, handrails, etc and the location of cream paintwork upon each. The addition of a life-guard rail to this one, however, follows 1930 legislation to that effect. The crew practise for the 'Ministry of Silly Walks', at Paul Street, Exeter, in 1935. *Royston Morgan / The Omnibus Society*

constituted Western National's territory, while in the north DGO&T's area was, for the time being, again pegged back to Tiverton.

Meanwhile events at a national level were destined to loosen NEC's direct control over the company's affairs. Although in 1928 NEC was not yet part of the British Electric Traction group, Tilling and BET holdings in territorial companies had been combined with the founding of the Tilling & British Automobile Traction Co Ltd. Tilling & BAT had negotiated a deal with the 'big four' British main-line railway companies whereby each of the latter would give up its own bus services and buy into the existing bus industry in its relative operating area. Thus, for instance, in the case of the westward-marching National Omnibus & Transport Co Ltd, those in the GWR area were destined to be subsumed under a new (and aforementioned) Western National Omnibus Co Ltd — whilst those, in the main, in the Southern Railway's domain were to become the concern of Southern National. Two directors of the appropriate railway joined the board of each bus company, and one third of the increased shares became the property of the relevant railway company.

The National Electric Construction Co decided to follow suit, and its subsidiaries became one-third-owned by railway companies.

Equivalent workhorse to the Leyland Titan at single-deck level was the
Leyland Lion. Fourteen of these LT1 models with Hall Lewis bodywork to
dual-doorway layout arrived with Devon General in 1930. No 157 (DV 4119)
was a 31-seat example, employed, in the main, upon the Exeter–Torquay
services, in this case via the seaside route. *Ian Allan Library*

In the case of Devon General both GWR and Southern Railway directors joined the board — in January 1930 — in the ratio of three (Lord Mildmay of Flete, James Milne and Richard H. Nicholls of the GWR) to two (Lt Col Gilbert S. Szlumper and D. S. McBright of the Southern). The Southern Railway quickly showed that it was basically 'friendly' by offering a site for a new garage at Exmouth — a 42-year lease at £85 per annum (steelwork by J. Partridge & Co Ltd for £530 and built by Abels for £2,590), which enabled the property at Exeter Road to be sold for £1,500.

Thus reinforced financially, DGO&T negotiated with Exeter Corporation for the tenancy of the bus station at Paul Street, Exeter, and put in train Daniel Campbell's plan to replace all the old high-framed vehicles with the low-loading types now on the market. It also planned a new service to Orcombe Point (which the Southern Railway advertised on its premises) and for £75 took over Mrs Searle's parcel agency 'twixt Budleigh Salterton town and railway station, buying two 12-seater Morris Commercial saloons to run passengers thence to local hotels.

The major undertaking of this period was the planning and erection of a central overhaul and repair depot cum garage on 3½ acres of land in Newton Road, Torquay, sold to DGO&T by one of its directors, Benjamin Stedham, for some £1,275 per acre. It was to be equipped to provide cover for an eventual 85 vehicles, together with five petrol pumps, Bowser tanks and one 2,000gal oil tank and pump. Whilst this was put in motion the long-desired garage at Moretonhampstead became a reality when land was bought there for £200 and H. Mills & Son of Newton Abbot were engaged to build it, in 11 weeks, for £2,925. Thus the company established an important interchange point in the upper reaches of the rivers Teign and Bovey ('Buvvey').

For several years a collection of local bus operators, mostly with just one vehicle apiece and protected to a certain extent by membership of the Torquay & District Motor Coach Owners' Association, competed along the southern coast of Torbay. DGO&T was said, rather romantically, to be 'concerned about the presence of pirates on the Paignton and Brixham Road' (and the Royal Navy had long since departed!). On 25 February 1931 it was announced that the last eight had surrendered, their licences and goodwill having been acquired for a total of £1,200. No vehicles were taken over.

The last act of the DGO&T under the self-governing NEC was to put in motion negotiations leading to the acquisition of Timpson & Sons' operations in Torquay (see Chapter 5). Arrangements for NEC and its territorial operating subsidiaries to be subsumed under the overall control of the British Electric Traction group had started in late 1931. On 23 March 1932 it was reported that the National Electric Construction Co Ltd would remove from its offices at Salisbury Square House to BET headquarters at 88 Kingsway, London WC2. The registered office of Devon General went with it; but every director appointed to the DGO&T board by BET from that time to the end of Devon General's active existence (care of the National Bus Company nearly 40 years later) would be recorded as nominally representing . . . NEC!

▲ Originally intended for limited-stop service use, this Leyland Lion LT2 with 31-seat Hall Lewis bodywork was photographed on rather more prosaic stage-carriage work in its later days and livery. No 172 (DV 5483) is pictured at Paul Street bus station, Exeter, ready for a short journey to Rockbeare Cross Roads. It also bears a short-lived route-number board on the dash. *J. F. Higham / A. B. Cross collection*

◄ Following the appointment to its board of representatives from the GWR and Southern Railway, Devon General took over the parcels agency at Budleigh Salterton, together with an operation between the town's hotels and the SR railway station. No 178 (DV 5834) was one of a pair of Morris Commercial/Hall Lewis 12-seaters dedicated to the task in 1930. *Calton Phoenix*

In 1931 Hall Lewis became 'Park Royal'. The reconstituted coachbuilder's first order from Devon General was for 20 dual-door saloons on Leyland Lion LT2 chassis. Tacked on to that order were four front-entrance-only examples built to coach specification, with the company's standard interior luggage rack at rear — Nos 21-4 (DV 8506-9), of which this was one. *Philip Platt collection*

In a change of tack Daniel Campbell recommended that 10 AEC Regal 26-seater coaches, primarily for limited-stop service, should be purchased. They arrived in 1931, fitted with Park Royal coachwork. Presumably with GWR, SR, Western National and Southern National approval No 180 (DV 9216) and its fellows served on joint 'Devon National' services as far afield as Ilfracombe, Bude, Clovelly, Lynton and Cheddar. *Mallory Saltmarsh collection*

Perhaps anxious about its none-too-successful Lion LT3 model, Leyland offered Devon General a special deal: 'We will take six of your old AEC single-deckers in part exchange for six LT3 chassis.' The company agreed, and Leyland threw in another as well. Park Royal built the bodywork, including coach seats and interior luggage rack at the rear, for 'limited stop' use. *Philip Platt collection*

Eight vehicles at the end of a batch of 1932 Weymann-bodied 31-seater saloons 'built to our own standard' were fitted with 'sunshine roofs' and coach-standard seats. The chosen livery was unusual but relatively short-lived: a black roof and rear dome in addition to its black waistband. Clearly the editor of Devon General's house magazine liked it, for it received a special mention. *Calton Phoenix*

Remembering its earlier NEC associations with Brush Coachworks at Loughborough, in 1932 Devon General took delivery of three 52-seater AEC Regent double-deckers fitted with Brush bodywork of lowbridge configuration. Venturing bravely out of the works without so much as a trade plate, one of them poses outside Woolworth's in Loughborough. *Colin Morris collection*

Purporting to demonstrate the value of its lowbridge configuration, one of the three Regents which became Nos 190-2 (OD 2260/59/61) in the Devon General fleet stands beneath an ample Loughborough bridge. The livery applied is the short-lived one whereby the red was confined to below the waistrail, with three black bands and 'broken-white' above. *Colin Morris collection*

For those who cannot remember what the lower saloon interior of a lowbridge bus looked like, here is a forward view in one of Devon General's trio of AEC Regent/Brush double-deckers. The reduction in height has been achieved by sinking the upstairs gangway into that bulging ceiling (upper right) —nicely placed for banging one's head when leaving the seats beneath. *Colin Morris collection*

The last order placed by Devon General before the British Electric Traction Co Ltd formally absorbed NEC — and thereby Devon General — was for three Leyland Cub KP3 canvas-roofed 'convertible' coaches with 20-seat bodywork by Weymann — destined to become a popular builder with Devon General. The Cubs were described as 'the ultimate in luxury'. *Calton Phoenix*

The land for building a central works — some 3½ acres — in Newton Road, Torquay, was sold to Devon General by one of its directors, Benjamin Stedham, in 1930. The Lambhill Ironworks of Glasgow won the contract for the supply of steelwork, whilst R. Wilkins & Sons Ltd was engaged to construct the building, which, in this first phase, opened the following year. *Ian Allan Library*

On 25 January 1933 the board decided to order 18 new
Leyland Lion LT5 chassis — 10 fitted with 'our own
standard 31-seat saloon bodies' (by Weymann) and eight
with 'sun-saloon roofs', for some £20,000 complete.
On the latter, numbered 63-70 (OD 5863-9, 6149),
the black waistband and rear dome of the 31-seaters was
extended along the length of the roof. As on other
'sun saloons' of the period the seating was reduced to
accommodate a luggage pen on the nearside rear corner.
Calton Phoenix

4. BET's Devon General

So, the National Electric Construction Co Ltd had become an 'intermediate' subsidiary of the British Electric Traction Co Ltd. An early task of the Devon General board under BET supervision was to finalise the £82,000 purchase of Grey Cars and Timpson's other operation, now known as the South Devon Motor Garage Co Ltd, and pay off the temporary loans for that purpose from the GWR (£30,000), Benjamin Stedham (£10,000) and Torquay Tramways (£5,000). To do so it arranged for additional share capital, raising this by £130,000 to £300,000. Sadly, this was agreed at the last meeting attended by William Cownie. He died on 4 December 1932, to be replaced as a director by Sidney Garcke, son of the founder of BET, Emile Garcke.

The first sign of dissent from railway-appointed directors came in January 1933, when the GWR 'looked into' the matter of a proposed new service from Newton Abbot to Hennock — odd! More likely to have disturbed them was the possibility of competition in the Torbay area from trolleybuses. The Torquay & Paignton Traction Bill had been presented to Parliament — its main concern a proposed replacement of the trams by a service of speedy trolleybuses. By that June Torquay Tramways had abandoned such an idea, however, and agreed that Devon General should operate a replacement service of motor buses on its behalf when the tramway was abandoned.

Throughout the previous 12 months Daniel Campbell had suffered ill health, eventually diagnosed as appendicitis. Despite an operation he felt unable to continue as General Manager, becoming instead a consultant for the company. Although he did not return to active service, happily he lived until 7 December 1962. Campbell was replaced by a Dubliner, Reginald Porte, previously Engineer for Southdown Motor Services Ltd, but his post with DGO&T was destined to be terminated 'by mutual consent' in November 1936.

Exactly three years earlier the DGO&T capital had been raised again (to £350,000), and £1,500 of the extra cash was used the following March (1934) to acquire the goodwill of the Sidmouth, Sidford and Exeter service of the Sidmouth Motor Bus Co. That purchase was followed by the Ottery St Mary–Exeter service of R. P. Summers, for £587 10s 0d. Attempting to start a service from Paignton to Collaton St Mary in May 1935, Devon General was met by an objection from Western National that this would compete with the latter's route to Totnes. Devon General consoled itself by acquiring A. C. Aggett's Marldon–Paignton service plus one Ford BB/Mumford 20-seater bus, for £800, and, in July, the goodwill of Milton's Services (Crediton) Ltd, for £1,875.

Long expected, in January 1936 the company grudgingly recognised the National Union of Railwaymen's right to represent its members in any dispute, grumbling that this would have the effect of granting a 48-hour week and that the payment of overtime for working in excess of 54 hours would cost it an additional £3,000 per annum. The following year the board was both surprised and grateful when the NUR chased its members at Exmouth and Sidmouth back to work within hours when they came out on unofficial strike because 'the new summer duties are too onerous'.

Another kind of 'joining up' soon followed. Again it was Germany that was causing alarm by its expansionist intent. On 30 March 1936 Harold Barnett agreed with Lt Col Likeman of the HQ Wessex Recruiting Area that Devon General employees should be enlisted into the Supplementary (Transport) Reserve — provided that attending training camp would not entail their absence from duty. Thus Devon General played its part in response to the 'Alarm Calls' three years prior to the outbreak of World War 2.

The spring of 1937 saw Reginald Porte's replacement by the appointment as Secretary and Manager of F. B. Low, followed by

Sidney Garcke, a director of Devon General from 1933, served as Chairman from 1942 to 1946 and could be considered the most 'high profile' to hold that office. The son of Emile Garcke, founder of the British Electric Traction Co Ltd, he convinced his father — by 1910 — that motor buses could be successful in their own right rather than used merely as feeders for tramway systems. *Colin Morris collection*

45

Backed up against the Marine Tavern in Palk Street, Torquay, are a pair of the two dozen AEC Regent O661s delivered in 1934 — the year Devon General began operating double-deckers in earnest. Fitted with 52-seat bodywork by Short Bros, they replaced the Torquay trams. The first diesel-engined vehicles in the fleet, rebuilt or rebodied examples served for up to 27 years with the company. Nos 211/23 (OD 7498, 7510) are in as-new livery. *Royston Morgan collection*

With its fleet number displayed fore and aft in an unusual and distinctly municipal style, No 74 (OD 9487) was one of three Leyland Lion LT5 saloons bodied by Brush in 1934 to a standard BET design. The three others of the same batch were bodied to the same pattern by Short Bros, each costing an estimated £1,000. No 74 was photographed in Loughborough prior to registration. *Colin Morris collection*

A rather splendid and ornate map dating from the mid-1930s. *Royston Morgan collection*

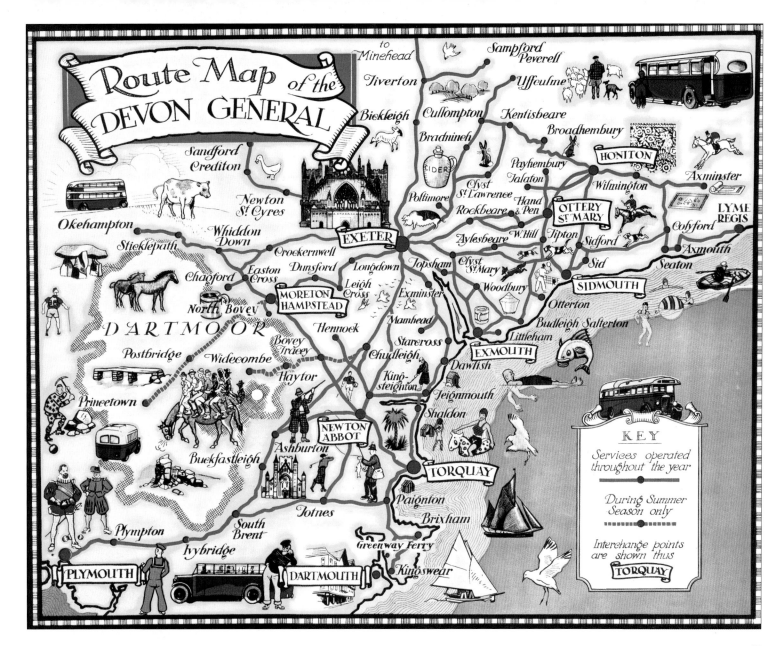

Working service 4 (Honiton–Ottery St Mary–Exeter) is No 77 (AUO 72), the first of Devon General's famous 'camels', photographed to best advantage to show off the type's peculiar roofline. This housed an especially large internal luggage rack. One of a batch of 18 with 36-seat Short bodywork, this Leyland Lion LT5A of 1935 is sandwiched between two Southern National saloons, with a Dodson-bodied AEC Reliance on the left.
The Omnibus Society

◄ In July 1936 Sidney Garcke was authorised to consider the type of chassis to be chosen for 48 saloon buses — the company's largest-ever batch. Pictured at work on service 6 (Exeter–Tedburn St Mary–Sticklepath–Okehampton) is No 296 (CTA 107), a diesel-engined Leyland Lion LT7 delivered in 1937. Unforttunately Garcke's choice seems to have been based upon price rather than performance, their four-cylinder units proving grossly underpowered for Devon's hills. All were fitted with 36-seat Harrington bodywork.
Alan Lambert collection

the purchase of the goodwill of Miller & Son's stage-carriage services at Exmouth. Oh, and the donation of 25 guineas (£26.25p) to Torquay United Football Club, for improvements at Plainmoor. Football had long been taken very seriously at Devon General.

As the clouds of war gathered, Torquay Corporation had adopted a rather hopeful stance about such things and prepared a plan to provide the town with a new bus station. This would have involved the demolition of a 160ft frontage in Vaughan Parade. That, of course, was the location of Devon General's tours office, which was being rented at £350 per annum. The actual outbreak of war in September 1939 put paid to the bus-station scheme, and it was never revived.

By the 25th of that first month of war the company's services had been reduced to 50% of a basic 'winter' operation. Some 100 members of staff had joined the military services. In consequence of that and the rationing of fuel Devon General pulled in its horns even further: the firm discharged up to 200 employees. Caught up in this was John 'Jack' Jarvis, a rare example of a native of Devon who rose through the ranks of Devon General to a top managerial appointment — that of Area Traffic Superintendent, Torbay, and finally District Manager with the new Devon General Ltd. Born in Yeoford, he had watched the Devon General buses going by his uncle's house at Newton St Cyres and decided 'That's for me!' Aged 18, he joined the company in the summer of 1939 and after three days was 'posted' as a conductor to Sidmouth. That didn't last long; he was an early victim of the heavy pruning. Since working the buses was declared a 'reserved occupation' the company realised that it had overdone things somewhat. At that early stage only one driver at Exeter — Bill Schofield — had been called to the colours, and that was because he was an Army reservist. Then, when conductors started to be called up,

the purchase for £150 of the goodwill of the stage-carriage business run by G. & W. Harris of Ipplepen. In the summer plans were put in train for the erection of a six-vehicle garage in Lodge Road, Tiverton, on land leased from the GWR. After a difficult discussion with Torquay Corporation about the use of Union Street by the company's buses and an attempt by the Council to pin the fares within the borough to a penny per mile the latter, at least, was resolved by the Traffic Commissioners for the Western Area at 1.1 pence per mile.

The year closed with a further territorial retraction, the goodwill of the Sidmouth–Beer–Seaton service (52) being sold to Southern National for a nominal consideration of £50. This was part of a revised territorial agreement between the two companies, signed on 20 January 1938.

Two noteworthy concerns for the directors during 1938 were the reversion to his role solely as Secretary of F. B. Low, leading to the appointment of a new General Manager, R. G. James, and

Until World War 2 put an end to the Ilsham Marine
Drive route — in Kilmorie, Thatcher and Hope Cove
territory — Bedford WTB No 360 (CTT 660), with
24-seat bodywork by Birch, was one of a pair dedicated
to the 'Coastal Cruise'. Dressed in duck-egg blue and
cream, with chromium trim, both had entered service
in June 1937 with unglazed side windows.
Calton Phoenix

In the late 1930s the cap badge for drivers and
conductors, with the word 'DEVON' (curved
downward) above 'GENERAL' (curved up),
was replaced by one featuring this elegant
crown motif. Perhaps inspired by the fleet's
AEC Regals and Regents, it was nevertheless
designed and made by jewellers Fatorini —
in Regent Street, Birmingham. This style of
badge was to survive until replaced, like
everything else, by the National Bus Company.
Colin Morris

Apparently pleased with the Birch bodywork on its first
(1937) pair of Bedfords, the company turned again to
that coachbuilder the following year for another brace
of Bedfords — 14-seaters on the lighter WLG chassis.
No M418 (EUO 192) and its stablemate were originally
intended for one-man working at Sidmouth but is seen
postwar as a 20-seater, bound for Dawlish.
Mallory Saltmarsh collection

the young Jarvis was reinstated for a year, until he too became
eligible — and joined the Royal Navy. Invalided out in 1944,
he rejoined Devon General for a second time, eventually taking
early retirement in 1983.

In 1940 the company dug trenches, built air-raid shelters for its
staff and bowed to the inevitable in employing conductresses,
whom it gallantly called 'girl conductors' and paid at the same
rate as the men — not usual in those days. April saw it buy the
goodwill of the services of W. J. Abbott (Exmouth) Ltd for
£2,600. In July some 48 vehicles from Devon General's largely
dormant fleet were requisitioned by the War Office, to be
followed by another pair that December, the company accepting
£20,000 and £1,416 respectively for the two batches.

The company's premises also attracted the attention of the
War Office. The top floor of Torwood Street garage, Torquay, was
occupied by the Air Ministry, and a portion of the lower became
an Air Raid Precautions gas-decontamination centre. The upper
portion and garage at Blackboy Road, Exeter, was leased to Air
Service Training Ltd. In order to cope with these disruptions

One of a batch of 32 Harrington bodied AEC Regals which marked the start of Devon General's policy of matching fleet and registration numbers. Like the majority of the batch SR431 (DDV 431) was a 35-seater; the first six were 32-seat 'sun saloons' of the newly introduced XR class. *Calton Phoenix*

On 11 January 1939 the Devon General board amended an earlier authorisation to purchase four six-cylinder-engined Leyland KPZ04 chassis to one for just two, at £535 each. Weymann's estimate of £451 was accepted, and M452 (DDV 452) and its companion duly entered service at Brixham on 1 June 1939. *Calton Phoenix*

Under an emergency scheme in June 1939, prior to the outbreak of World War 2, Devon General converted six 1938 AEC Regal/Harrington saloons — including SR408 (DUO 320) — into ambulances for the Royal Naval Authorities. The work involved the removal of seats and their replacement by cot and stretcher-case accommodation, with access by means of the specially built ramp. *Calton Phoenix*

Who could argue with these two? 'Girl Conductors', as Devon General gallantly dubbed them, were first employed in 1940, as a wartime emergency measure. The same rates of pay and conditions of service — if not hours of duty — applied to them as to male conductors. Both summer and winter outfits are modelled here, whilst the driver appears to have his hands clasped in prayer. But with hats worn at a jaunty angle — like Earl Beatty's at the Battle of Jutland — who could doubt the outcome? *Calton Phoenix*

Devon General established what turned out to be the precursor of a much later relationship with Court Garages (Torquay) Ltd when it temporarily leased from that firm its garage in Belgrave Road. In a move clearly arranged by Sidney Garcke, the secretarial office of the company removed to Ditton House, Maidenhead, Berkshire, previously the celebrated house of BET's founder, his father Emile.

In the autumn of 1940 the company gained permission to operate double-deckers through to Brixham and, because of the increased evacuee population in the Torbay area, found itself short of such vehicles. Five East Kent Leyland Titans, prised from Southdown, which had borrowed them previously, arrived to relieve the situation — at £3 each per day.

As Luftwaffe air raids seemed likely to come its way Devon General arranged to disperse its vehicles. Eighteen from Exeter were allotted places at Pocombe Quarry, whilst room for 20 Torquay buses was found in a disused brickworks and rubbish tip near Lawes Bridge, Newton Road. A spine-chilling order, proclaimed in July 1941, stated that the company's Home Guard platoon, formed in June 1940, should — in the event of 'Action

One of a pair of 8.8-litre AEC Regent O661s delivered in 1937 with metal-framed Weymann bodywork seating 57 passengers, DR235 (DTT 48) has a good load of passengers aboard at Brixham. It is dressed in full World War 2 garb — masked lights, white wingtips and with lower-deck band in grey; but, to give the Luftwaffe a sporting chance, the roof remains cream!
S. L. Poole / London Bus Preservation Group / Royston Morgan collection

In November 1937 an order was placed for 25 Dennis four-cylinder-diesel-engined chassis at £690 each — with an £18 rebate if three were taken 'as soon as possible'; there was a promise that, if these proved unsuitable, Devon General could cancel the remaining 22 chassis. Thus the company took delivery of just SD298-300, Dennis Lancet IIs with 35-seat Harrington bodywork. This wartime view features SD298 (DUO 330) at Castle Circus, Torquay.
The Omnibus Society

Stations' being called — man road blocks near Newton Road garage, instead of defending the garage itself; a separate platoon of drivers and buses was earmarked to provide Army transport in such an event. Such was the paucity of suitable vehicles from any other source that January 1942 saw the hire of two London Transport ST-class double-deckers, for one year, at £25 per vehicle per month.

Finding the going a little too hot elsewhere, the Luftwaffe came instead for the 'soft' target of Exeter on 4 May 1942. Much of the beautiful old mediæval city was wrecked. 'Exeter was a jewel — and we have destroyed it,' boasted Goebbels' propaganda ministry. Well . . . not entirely, but that night 16 Devon General employees had their homes completely or partially destroyed. On 1 July a company fitter lost his at Teignmouth, and another suffered likewise at St Marychurch on 4 September, in a raid which demolished a church and killed several Sunday-school children.

As the tide of war began to turn so the need to save fuel for military purposes became paramount. A trial Enniss Sentinel 'Victory' gas-producer unit was fitted to General Manager R. G. James' Wolseley car, followed in April-June 1943 by the purchase of 23 Bristol-built 'T2'-type producer-gas trailer units, at approximately £100 each, for fitment to the rear of several company omnibuses. In hilly Devon particularly such things were not a great success, and buses so equipped held up following military convoys

rather than being of much help to the war effort. Nevertheless, such buses saw service to Newton Abbot and Kingsteignton, for instance, where the road at Sandygate Cross was widened to enable them to turn around without reversing. The use of producer gas for buses was abandoned in November 1944.

Rather belatedly, in 1943, Devon General decided to disperse further vehicles on land it had recently purchased at Marsh Barton Lane, on the outskirts of Exeter. Fortunately that move proved unnecessary, but at the time . . . Such was the build-up in the area of the military's own transport facilities, particularly those of the United States Army, that Devon General began to reacquire several of its previously requisitioned vehicles, which required sprucing up somewhat before returning to service.

Whilst Exeter City Council helped Devon General with its accommodation difficulties — by renting out part of its Paris Street garage and extending the lease of Paul Street bus station —

Oh, I do like to be beside the seaside . . . even if it's a grey winter's day. Cruising south along Torbay Road, DG318 (ETX 832) was one of a pair of Guy Arab/Weymann 56-seaters that had started life with fellow BET subsidiary Rhondda and came to Devon in 1944 as part of an in-house exchange deal involving the two Daimler CWG5s, considered more suited to the Welsh company.
Royston Morgan collection

For reasons not satisfactorily explained the local vehicle-registration office got its numbers considerably out of sequence in 1942/3; 'JTA' appeared some five years ahead of schedule, so the main batch of Guy Arab/Weymann utilities arrived thus registered. In all-over grey, DG314 (JTA 314) was suitably dressed to avoid attention from the Luftwaffe whilst on a Torquay local service in September 1943.
S. L. Poole / London Bus Preservation Group

Newton Abbot Urban District Council served notice that the use of the town's Market Square as a bus station was to come to an end. The board found it necessary to remind the council of its responsibility to help the company provide an essential facility for the public and to aid the search for an alternative site. Possibly buoyed up by Victory in Europe (1945), the Newton Abbot councillors came around to agreeing a five-year extension to the existing arrangements. It was to last rather longer than that.

As World War 2 came to a close there were two resignations of particular note from the Devon General board — the original GWR director, Lord Mildmay of Flete, and Brigadier Sir Bruce White KBE, his knighthood conferred in recognition of his role in the provision of the prefabricated Mulberry Harbour used after the D-Day landings in 1944.

In 1946, that first year of an austerity-constrained peace, John Spencer Wills — an important figure in the annals of BET history — joined the Devon General board, and Harold Barnett, after 24 years as a director, retired. Negotiations with Exeter City Council led to an agreement, on 11 January 1947, for the joint operation of services within the city and on a defined number of routes around it, on the basis of an equal division of the pooled receipts and of the mileage operated in that area. Five directors, with three in reserve, became members of the joint committee set up to administer the arrangements, which, in the event, were to last for 24 years. Thus the green vehicles of Exeter were to be seen running beyond the city boundaries as far out as Dunchideock, Heath Cross, Crediton, Shobrooke, Upton Pyne, Cullompton, Poltimore and Exmouth. In exchange red Devon General buses operated on 11 city services using the Corporation's identifying route letters.

As this got underway both Exeter and the two National companies gave Devon General the go-ahead to gain some ground to the northwest of Tiverton. This was achieved by the purchase, for £3,195, of the stage-carriage services of Greenslades Tours Ltd in the Exeter, Crediton, Witheridge and Tiverton areas. Both Southern National (£1,100) and Western National (£95) agreed to participate in that purchase, in proportion to those services which could be adjusted to suit their purposes. This led to the setting up of a Devon General outstation-cum-depot at Witheridge, in the care, initially, of Inspector Tucker.

Talks with the GWR commenced in January 1947 with a view to developing a car park in Paignton for use as a bus station. Paignton Urban District Council and Western National became involved in the discussions, the latter becoming a partner in the project. However, it was Mother Nature, in the form of an unexpectedly high water table, which proved a major but eventually surmountable stumbling block. In 1955 the now 'British Railways' accepted £3,250 each from both companies for the purchase of the site. In July 1959 the plans were ready, and the projected cost, to be shared between the two, was £38,500; construction actually got underway in January 1960. When Inspector H. Luke was appointed to take charge for Devon General at Paignton bus station it had become the longest-running project in which the company had been involved. Its status was upgraded in July 1966 when it was added to the official list of

'depots', bringing the total number to eight. The remarkable thing is that (in 2006) it is still in full use.

Back in 1947, when the saga began, there were important changes at senior-officer level. First, H. C. Manley was replaced as Chief Engineer by Gerald Sedgwick. Then J. Spencer Wills, who had been Chairman for just one year, was replaced in that role by William Thomas James. He had been, in 1922, a co-founder of Lewis & James of Newbridge, West Mon, which firm had been purchased by South Wales Commercial Motors, a subsidiary of . . . the National Electric Construction Co Ltd. He had just about time to shake hands with R. G. James, the General Manager, when the latter, in turn, was replaced by Arthur J. White, originally with White's Motors, of Barry. The Celts had returned in force.

In September 1949 began the long and, at first, frustrating story of the West Exe railway bridge, on the southern outskirts of Tiverton. The raised camber of the road beneath had reduced the clearance to below the statutory 15ft. Lowering that surface would involve the co-operation of the bus operators, the Railway Executive and Devon County Council. The response of the latter to

Brought out of storage following World War 2, the two 'Coastal Cruise' Bedford WTBs were suitably converted for rather more prosaic duties as 20-seat, one-man operated country buses. A suitable example is the now M361 (CTT 661), painted in traditional Devon General livery and photographed in August 1952 on service from Dawlish to Langdon Barton and Ashcombe Church. *Alan B. Cross*

correspondence upon the matter was . . . silence! Frustrated indeed, Devon General received from Leyland Motors an offer of six lowbridge double-deckers, for early delivery at the special price of £3,450 each, and accepted it, safe in the belief that where three AEC Regents of 1932 had succeeded, so too could these new Leylands.

The matter was finally resolved by the raising of the bridge by the Railway Executive (Western Region), aided by a grant from the Ministry of Transport; the cost of the operation, completed in July 1952, was shared between Devon General (£840), the Railway Executive (£560) and Devon County Council (£700). Highbridge buses could now operate on the route, and the lowbridge Leyland PD2s were free to work elsewhere.

A much less painful exercise concerned the replacement of a bridge over the road running between two portions of the Earl of Devon's estate at Powderham Castle, and double-deck services commenced running on that road from 25 March 1951. At around the same time permission was granted for the operation of double-deck buses from Sidmouth — save upon the route to Exmouth. On 1 June 1952 Devon General took over the Exmouth–Otterton–Ladram Bay service, purchased for £15,000 from Mrs W. A. Hart of Budleigh Salterton, together with five single-deck vehicles (which it did not use). In the same month the company agreed to contribute £250 toward the cost of lowering the road beneath Kersbrook railway bridge at

On a summer's-day trip from Babbacombe to Paignton DG325 (GTT 425), one of six Guy Arab II/Park Royal 56-seat utilities of 1944, gets away from the Grand Hotel stop in Torbay Road. Although rebuilt in 1947 it retained its basic profile until withdrawal in 1959. It is closely followed here by AEC Regent DR220, as rebodied by Brush in 1949. *J. Bamsey / Royston Morgan collection*

East Budleigh, to permit the use of double-deckers on service 40 between Exmouth and Sidmouth.

There followed a clutch of stage-carriage service acquisitions: two from Newton Abbot, to Shaldon and to Maidencombe, together with one saloon bus, for £4,250 from Ball's Bus Services Ltd on 2 November 1952 (for the later acquisition of that firm's tours business see Chapter 5), two from Bishopsteignton, to Teignmouth and to Newton Abbot, plus one 20-seater coach, for £6,000 from H. D. Gourd & Sons, and another two from the Sidmouth Motor Co & Dagworthy Ltd for £2,000 — Sidmouth–Salcombe Regis (122) and Sidmouth–Peak Hill (123) — on 4 June 1956.

BET having moved its headquarters from 88 Kingsway WC2 to Stratton House, Piccadilly W1, on 17 March 1952, the registered office of Devon General went with it. The latter was removed again, to 87 Newton Road, Torquay, on 1 May 1956. That summer the estimated cost of a

At 7.10pm on an evening in August 1952 lowbridge all-Leyland Titan PD2/1 DL641 (MTT 641) pauses in Broad Street, Lyme Regis, on a limited-stop run between Weymouth and Exeter. Those people ignoring it are awaiting a Southern National for Crewkerne. *Colin Morris*

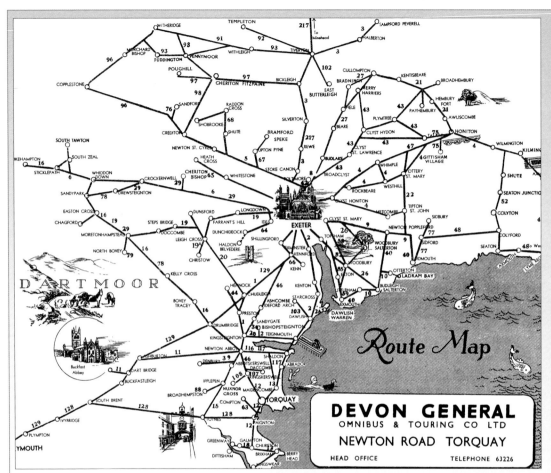

Map of Devon General routes *c*1953.

A rear view, for a change — Leyland Royal Tiger PSU1/9 SL636 (MTT 636) taking a rest inside Newton Road depot; it was one of five, with Willowbrook bodywork, delivered in 1951. When, three years later, that little disc (this one green) was affixed below the service-number box, it denoted to which garage the bus 'belonged'.
Philip Platt collection

Ugly duckling turned swan. Representing the numerous Devon General vehicles that gained an extra lease of life with new bodywork is Guy Arab DG248 (JTA 548), one of 17 wartime buses rebodied in 1951 by Roe. Each also received a Guy 'Feathers in our cap' radiator badge, so attractive that many fell victim to theft. *Ian Allan Library*

The first 8ft-wide double-deckers: one of a batch of 14 delivered in 1951, DR658 (MTT 658) was an AEC Regent III with 56-seat Weymann bodywork. Photographed in 1963, it was still putting in a hard day's work on the route to Newton Abbot via Teignmouth. *Royston Morgan*

Added to the tail end of the 20-strong 1952 batch of AEC Regent IIIs was one which — outwardly, at least — differed from the rest. This was DR679 (NTT 679), its trial Weymann 'Aurora' body featuring that builder's first 'tin front' concealing the radiator. For exhibition purposes it was given this special livery, but once in Torquay it had its cream areas 'restored' to their rightful Devon General places. *Ian Allan Library*

In 1952, as part of its investigation of lightweight vehicles, Devon General married the chassis of a 1937 AEC Regent with parts from a 1938 Regal and had the result fitted with a 56-seat body by Saunders-Roe. The combination weighed just 5 tons 19cwt, of which just under 2 tons was attributable to the aluminium-alloy bodywork. The registration carried here found its way onto a Grey Cars coach, and the rebuild entered service (in 1953) as DR705 (ETT 995). *Ian Allan Library*

In the early 1950s Devon General conducted a programme of cannibalisation, fitting engines etc from redundant AEC Regals to second-hand Regent chassis acquired from AEC. Weymann built the bodies, and the buses were dubbed 'Light Sixes'. DR720 (DDV 423) was one of the last five, 'new' in 1954, fitted with distinctive front wings. *Geoff Rixon*

In Fleet Street, Torquay, and bound for St Marychurch on a local service is DR700 (DJF 326), an AEC Regent O661 of 1946 — one of six received in 1952 from Leicester Corporation as part of an exchange deal. Difficulty with the destination layout on its 56-seat Park Royal body saw it remodelled Devon General-style soon after. *Geoff Rixon*

In 1955, in line with a national trend among bus companies within a suitably
attractive terrain, Devon General had the tops lopped off five AEC Regents
of 1934 vintage and reversed the livery, so that cream predominated.
To add to the 'vintage' appearance route boards at the sides were reintroduced.
Nos DR203/18 (OD 7490, 7505) pass at Babbacombe on summer services
to Broadsands and Kingswear respectively. *S. J. Butler collection*

The 12 Weymann-bodied AEC Regent IIIs (type 9613S) delivered in 1954 were known affectionately as 'Fire Engines' on account of their excellent performance with 9.6-litre engines. Having lost its 'DR' prefix in 1962, 732 (PDV 732) leaves Exeter, passing the once popular ABC cinema *en route* for Sidmouth, in May 1964. Sadly, neither bus nor cinema remains with us. *Royston Morgan*

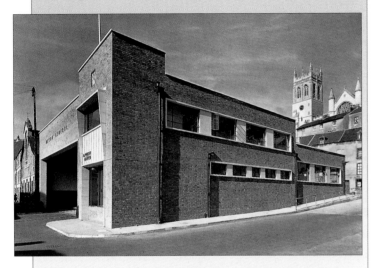

After several failed attempts to establish a depot at Brixham, Devon General eventually succeeded in opening this one in 1957, on the site of an old malthouse purchased from Brixham UDC. How the architect, W. E. Gott, managed to utilise the terrain and match the perpendicular structure of much older buildings is displayed here to good effect. The property comprised a bus station-cum-garage, enquiry office, cafeteria and offices. *Ian Allan Library*

With registration numbers carrying on from a batch of Beadle-Commer integral coaches came a similar number (six) turned out by Beadle as service buses of 7ft 6in width. No SC759 (ROD 759), delivered in 1956, was a 40-seater. *P. Yeomans / Royston Morgan collection*

combined garage and bus station at Brixham had risen from £10,000 to three times that figure — and the company set about arranging with Exeter Corporation what turned out to be a £2,250-per-annum rental for the use of the new bus station to be erected in Paris Street, Exeter.

In keeping with BET's promotional system, whereby managers of perceived distinction moved up the ladder to larger subsidiaries, Arthur White became General Manager of Maidstone & District Motor Services Ltd, in April 1957. He was replaced by Thomas L. C. Strange, destined to become the last General Manager of an active Devon General Omnibus & Touring Co Ltd. One of Tom Strange's more satisfying tasks was to oversee

arrangements for the replacement of prefabricated buildings at Newton Abbot by a new purpose-built bus station. Thus Newton Abbot quietly usurped Kingsteignton's role as a 'depot', property there being sold to British Road Services in November 1960. Being another football fanatic, Strange also saw to it that Devon General provided the coach for Torquay United's away games. Other members of the company's 'final team' began to take their seats when William Dravers replaced W. T. James as Chairman, on 26 September 1959.

From April 1963 until the matter was resolved in November 1967 Exeter Corporation's contribution to joint working within the city was in some trouble. The city wished to raise the fares within its boundaries to make good a shortfall in revenue. Eventually the Traffic Commissioners approved a joint increase on the lettered services and on the joint services in the whole of the extended city, to include Alphington, Pinhoe and Topsham, in respect of adult fares.

August 1964 saw the issue of £250,000 distributed as capital among the holders of the issued £1 million ordinary stock, in unissued shares of £1 each. At board meetings it became increasingly apparent that the British Transport Commission (railway) representatives were becoming agitated about decisions to loan surplus funds to bodies which, it seemed to them, were inappropriate, such diverse examples as the London Borough of Wandsworth, the Borough of Pembroke and the Borough of Gosport having been among the happy recipients. The BTC view was that such loans should be restricted to other BET subsidiaries.

When Transport Minister Barbara Castle announced the setting up of large territorial Passenger Transport Authorities — 'to cover the whole country', as the Devon General BET directors believed, somewhat prematurely (and to which they voiced their opposition) — Leonard Mapleston, representing the interim Government-inspired Transport Holding Company, repeated his warning, already issued to the board of the Trent Motor Traction Co (and others), that 'the THC cannot be associated with anti-Government propaganda'. The proverbial writing was upon the wall. Devon General was about to join other operators already fully nationalised.

On 22 November 1967 the British Electric Traction Co Ltd announced its (reluctant) agreement for the sale to the THC of its UK bus operations. Accordingly the whole of the ordinary stock held by the National Electric Construction Co Ltd and its nominees was transferred to the THC on 1 March 1968. Devon General's 'wayward' loans were promptly called in — no matter how much profit they had engendered.

On 20 November 1968, Tom Strange announced his resignation with effect from 31 January 1969. Others followed suit: William Dravers resigned from the board, Gerald Sedgwick, Chief Engineer, retired on 30 September, and the year closed with the resignation upon retirement of Noel Folkard, Traffic Superintendent, after 23 years in that role.

The newly formed National Bus Company filled the vacancies at senior level, and new Articles of Association led to the transfer of Devon General's registered office to National House, Queen Street, Exeter — home of the Western National Omnibus Co Ltd. It was from there that the 'sale' to the Devon General Omnibus & Touring Co Ltd of the assets of the Exeter City Transport undertaking for £190,000, plus the lease of its garage and offices at Heavitree Road, Exeter, at a rent of £5,000 per annum, was negotiated.

With effect from 1 January 1971 the operations of the Devon General Omnibus & Touring Co Ltd, the brainchild of John Stuart Mill the younger, were transferred to Western National. The company became 'dormant' but, as far as Companies House is concerned, still lives, as Chapter 6 will reveal.

No 799 (VDV 799) and its companion here were part of a batch of AEC Reliance MU3RA models with 41-seat bodywork by Weymann. Fitted, for one-man operation, with NCR equipment, they acquired the nickname 'Flying cash machines'. Pictured in July 1968, 799 was doubling up on a Torbay local service to Paignton. *Photobus*

Taking a rest at Newton Abbot bus station in between duties as a local-service vehicle, No 864 (864 ATA) was a 1959 AEC Reliance 2MU3RV with 41-seat bodywork built by Willowbrook to standard BET specification. *Philip Platt collection*

Devon General purchased its first Albion Nimbus saloons — six of the NS3N model — in 1958. It seems remarkable that 31 passengers could find seats in them. Bodywork was by Willowbrook. No 841 (XTA 841) departs Newton Abbot on a Saturday journey to Hennock in 1969. *Royston Morgan*

One of a batch of 23 Leyland Atlantean PDR1/1 double-deckers with 75-seat bodywork by Roe delivered in 1960, 916 (916 DTT) was travelling along Torbay Road toward the stop for Torquay station, on service 12 for Newton Abbot, when photographed in July 1969. *Arnold Richardson / Photobus*

In a pleasant, symmetrical composition at Newton Abbot bus station Leyland Atlantean 875 (875 ATA) departs on an all-the-way service to Brixham. Very much a company which favoured the AEC Regent, Devon General turned to the rear-engined Atlantean in 1959, this example being one of its first, bodied by Metro-Cammell. *Royston Morgan*

Royal Blue coaches abound, together with a Black & White from Cheltenham, in Exeter's Paris Street coach station as Devon General 943 (943 HTT), an AEC Regent V/Weymann of 1962, pauses on Exeter joint city service S, to High Meadows. *Royston Morgan collection*

The driver catches up on the daily news aboard an Albion Nimbus NS3AN with 31-seat Harrington bodywork — a none-too-common combination. One of three such vehicles, delivered in 1962, 958 (958 HTT) has yet to have its blind changed for a journey from Teignmouth to Newton Abbot in June 1970. *Royston Morgan collection*

◄ Launched with considerable ceremony in 1961, nine Atlantean PDR1/1 buses with removable tops to their 75-seat Metro-Cammell bodywork were named after Devon's 'Sea Dogs'. At the height of summer *Admiral Blake*, *Sir Walter Raleigh* and *Sir Richard Grenville* are on patrol at the Pavilion, Torquay. *Calton Phoenix*

▲ How on earth could the Torquay Tramways' Dolter system have coped with this? A remarkable photograph of a high tide plus gale shows a non-convertible Atlantean bravely following 'Sea Dog' *Sir Richard Grenville* into the raging waters, which are clearly threatening the Spanish Barn, out of view to the left. *Torquay Times / Calton Phoenix collection*

New in 1964, 506 (506 RUO) was one of a batch
of eight AEC Regent V 2D3RAs with 69-seat
bodywork by Willowbrook. Here it awaits the off
in Vaughan Parade, Torquay, on the famous
route 12 — the section in this case being
the run to Newton Abbot, along the A380,
via Kingkerswell and Milber. *Royston Morgan*

Rolling along past the entrance to Palk Street, Torquay, against a background Napoleon himself would have admired— properties clinging to the rocks on Warren Hill — comes 14 (14 RDV), a 41-seat Willowbrook-bodied AEC Reliance 2MU3RA. New in 1964, the bus is on the anti-clockwise Inner Circle service. *Ian Allan Library*

Awaiting customers in the Strand, Torquay, is No 20 (CTT 20C) on the local service to Warberry Road. This saloon bus is a Reliance 2MU3RA with 41-seat bodywork by Park Royal, one of a batch of six delivered in 1965. *Philip Platt collection*

73

Delivered in 1965, the order for bodywork to be fitted to a dozen new AEC Regent V chassis was divided equally between Park Royal and Willowbrook. No 510 (CTT 510C), with 2D3RA chassis, was bodied by the former as a 69-seater, whereas the Willowbrook body on 520 (CTT 520C), a 2MD3RA model, seated 59, as befitted its shorter length. *Omnicolour; Royston Morgan*

Pictured at Newton Abbot, with a full load aboard, bound for the charmingly named Ipplepen — and on to Totnes — on service 15, is No 41 (HOD 41E). The vehicle is an AEC Reliance with bodywork built by Marshall to special Devon General requirements, including a short, swept-up stern. *Philip Platt collection*

What turned out to be the last batch of Leyland Atlanteans delivered to Devon General, in 1968/9, comprised 10 buses fitted with MCW bodywork, completed by Saunders Roe on Anglesey. These also featured the more powerful 680 engine in order to cope with hilly Torquay's local services. No 541 (NDV 541G) is pictured passing the Mallock Memorial Clock Tower. *Omnicolour / Royston Morgan collection*

Described in the order book for June 1968 as a 'BET standard with Devon General extras', AEC Reliance 505 6MU3R, with Marshall 'bus-grant' bodywork, No 73 (OTA 73G) is seen minus red roof-stripe at Newton Abbot bus station in 1970. The 'Decoy' destination is a reminder of much earlier wildfowling activities in that location.
Royston Morgan

With its 'snag-list' still on the windscreen, AEC Reliance 74 (TUO 74J) is driven out of the Willowbrook factory by that firm's Chief Inspector, Graham Unwin. The bus is in 'show model' condition, but the advertisement-panel area is already prepared. Unusually, these last Reliances emerged with red wheels, but these were repainted 'proper black' before entry into service.
Royston Morgan

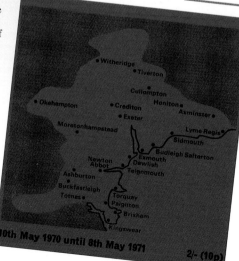

Timetable
Bus, Coach and Rail

Devon General
OMNIBUS & TOURING Co Ltd

10th May 1970 until 8th May 1971

2/- (10p)

▲ Most of the transferred Exeter Corporation vehicles retained their previous owner's attractive green livery. Formerly Exeter 59, 259 (UFJ 299), a 1957-vintage Guy Arab IV 6LW with 57-seat Park Royal body, is here operating on joint service 65 to Heath Cross via Whitestone. *Philip Platt collection*

▲ Ordered by Exeter but delivered in Devon General colours was No 218 (VOD 218K), one of seven Leyland Panther PSUR1B/1R models with 47-seat Marshall bodywork. *Royston Morgan collection*

Working the Exeter–Crediton–Sandford service is No 91 (VOD 91K), one of half a dozen Bristol LHS6L saloons with Marshall bodywork, the order switched, as elsewhere, from ECW. The design was unusual in that the windscreen frame was identical to the rearward-facing assembly. *Philip Platt collection*

▲ The last orders approved by an 'independent' board of directors — at the behest of the National Bus Company in 1970 — included nine Bristol VRs with 70-seat Eastern Coach Works bodywork, at £9,380 each. Delivered in 1971 to Western National (albeit in full Devon General livery), 549 (VOD 549K) was a classic NBC-era double-deck workhorse. *Royston Morgan*

5. Coaching

At the turn of the 19th/20th century tours to the delights of Dartmoor etc were horse-drawn. This small charabanc has come to a brief halt at the Haytor Rock Hotel, probably on a return trip from Widecombe in the Moor. The nearside horse looks worried by a strange-looking dog. *Colin Morris collection*

▼ The diverse and impressive character of the beauteous Devon countryside and coast has been outlined in Chapter 1. Wagonettes, charabancs and brakes drawn by a minimum of two horses apiece had long provided tourists and — to a lesser extent — local people with a means of getting out and about in this breathtaking environment.

When mechanical power arrived to relieve the horses from their labours the traffic increased markedly. Because of the outstanding attractiveness of the countryside thereabout Chagford, in particular, became a sought-after destination. To a considerable extent the timetabled journeys to the village by rival LSWR and GWR omnibuses had been for the benefit of tourists to see 'Chaggyvord, an' what d'ye think on't?' — and hear this proud local enquiry. And answer, of course, in the positive.

The GWR is said to have run the first motor-bus outing across Dartmoor (from its base in Paignton), but, bearing in mind the continuing practice of celebrating the totally false notion that Thomas Elliott started 'the' Royal Blue with a fleet of stage coaches in 1880, I have become somewhat sceptical about 'firsts' (see *Glory Days: Royal Blue*, Chapter 1). However, John Cummings (1980) has chronicled early touring activities of the GWR in the area with convincing detail, and Roger Grimley has written much about those who were genuine Devon-based operators in the area (see Bibliography).

The starting-points for much of the local tourist traffic were Newton Abbot, Paignton and Torquay. If the GWR was first with motor wagonettes and charabancs as early as 1904, it was closely followed by local proprietors. Torquay & District got off the mark with a Clarkson charabanc in 1905, while R. Coombes' 'Paignton & District' had two steam and two petrol-engined vehicles in use by 1908 — the same year that George Senior, of 5 Market Street, Torquay, began a small-scale operation.

As more reliable vehicles became available R. H. Grist — an established post-, job- and riding master of 3 Lisburne Square, Torquay — bought himself a couple of Commer 22-seat 'toastracks'. From 1911 he joined forces with W. R. Cutchey, T. Crossman, W. P. Hardy and W. Farrant Gilley to form the South Devon Garage & Motor Touring Co Ltd, which firm had eight vehicles in service before World War 1 put a temporary halt to its activities. The same befell the smaller operators in the area, among them W. E. Cawdle's 'Royal Blue' (no, not Elliott's) of Tor Church Road, A. Comley's Torquay & Dartmoor Touring Co and F. W. Humber's Cream Torpedo Cars — a name destined to outlast Devon General. It was the company founded upon Grist's business — and later chaired by W. R. Cutchey — that was destined to play a large part in the Devon General story.

Both horses and motor vehicles were requisitioned for the military during World War 1, while those motors left behind were subject to severe petrol rationing. What trips there were prolonged the use of horse-drawn vehicles, usually restricted to a 50-mile round-trip into Dartmoor or down to Slapton Sands.

By the 1920 season the availability of war-surplus vehicles — usually AEC, Daimler and Leyland, on solid or super-cushion tyres — had got things moving again. As elsewhere the first pneumatic tyres were tried out on small charabancs — the first in Torquay (or so they said) being a Garford of White Heather Tours, Babbacombe. Italy having been aligned with the Allies in World War 1, Lancia chassis had been available in the UK from 1915, the Triota of 1921 and the Tetraiota (1922-4) becoming very popular in the Torbay area with several operators, who were able to charge slightly higher fares because tourists liked the added comfort of their pneumatic tyres fitted as standard. Lancias were bought by White Heather, followed by Ruby Cars, Glorious Devon Cars, Royal Tours and Cawdle's Royal Blue. By 1922 most of the Paignton firms, including Zomba Cars, Reliance Cars and Comfy Cars, were on pneumatics. Hampton Cars at Torquay ran on both types, but in 1922 Victory Tours, Primrose Char-a-bancs and Captain Hutt's Fleet Cars Ltd, all with larger-type vehicles, were running on 'super cushion' tyres (solid, but with a cavity running around the centre section). The last-named firm, run by ex-Army men, used the subtitle 'The Ex-Service Service' on its nine yellow Dennis 28-seat coaches.

Earlier the South Devon Garage & Motor Touring Co Ltd had painted its vehicles pale grey and called its tours business 'The Grey Torpedo Cars', retaining the 'South Devon' name for local services and garage facilities. After World War 1 a separate company — The Grey Cars Ltd — was formed for the tours and excursions work. In 1922 the fleet consisted of nine AEC or Leyland 28-seaters and six 20-seat Daimlers, four of which were on pneumatics. In support of its excursions, from Paignton primarily, it also ran a stage-carriage service from Brixham.

When Devon General was amalgamated with the Torquay Tramways fleet in 1922 some 20 charabancs were available for the enlarged company's use, against which the rest — in the main — struggled to compete for the highly seasonal custom. In 1924 Devon General began the process of absorbing some of the survivors.

First to fall was Fleet Cars of Torwood Street, with four Stockport-registered Dennis 30-seaters and one Lancia, together with the remaining assets, by acquisition of its share capital for £4,000. Devon General changed the fleet livery to its own dark red and set about adding to the fleet 15 of the

new Lancia Pentaiota model, with 20-seat locally-built bodywork, five of which were in service by April 1925.

The Primrose Char-a-bancs Co having folded, DGO&T acquired its garage next to the Tramway car sheds at Preston, Paignton (which it promptly extended for Fleet Cars use), in May 1925 and that summer received a loan of £7,236 from Torquay Tramways to cover the purchase of Comfy Cars, which was run as a separate fleet during the 1926 summer season; an interesting vehicle which joined Devon General from this source was a 1923 Maxwell 14-seat coach, TA 5449. Receipts from the 1926 season were: Fleet Cars £15,557; Comfy Cars £6,057.

Next to surrender its licences, for £1,200, was White Heather. The two Lancia charabancs acquired went into the DGO&T fleet, but its premises were allotted to Fleet Cars Ltd, which remained a separate subsidiary. When the Great Western Railway representatives joined the Devon General board in 1930 they expressed a mild flutter of concern about the advertising of tours and private-hire trips in the Torquay area, but nothing much seems to have changed. In his proposed rolling-stock programme for 1931 Daniel Campbell outlined his plan for the replacement of the old

charabancs with modern coaches, and as part of that programme it was decided to order four additional Leyland Lions as coaches, in preference to overhauling six 1925 Dennis saloon buses.

As described in *Glory Days: Royal Blue* (2000), railway directors tended to exercise a degree of separateness on bus-company boards, and this led, in January 1931, to Devon General, at the request of the Southern Railway, co-operating with Greyhound Motors Ltd of Bristol to compete with Elliott Bros's Royal Blue on one of that firm's original routes; Devon General ran an express service between Torquay and Bournemouth, where passengers transferred to a Greyhound coach running between Bournemouth and London . . . until, that is, July of that year, when the Traffic Commissioners refused to renew the licences, granting them instead to a relieved Elliott Bros. Ironically, eight years later the Leyland Tiger coaches used by Devon General for this act of 'piracy' were sold to Western and Southern National for use on Royal Blue express services.

In September 1931 there was talk of a requirement for new coaches to be used for the Fleet Cars operation, but this was put on hold as a much bigger fish swam within reach. As early as November 1924 there had been a direct enquiry as to whether DGO&T might like to acquire Grey Cars and its allied South Devon Motor Garage Co. The offer was repeated — and again turned down — in January 1930. Instead, A. Timpson & Sons Ltd of Catford stepped in (as it did also at Hastings; see *Glory Days: Maidstone & District*) to purchase both, modernising the Grey Cars fleet and building a two-tier garage in Torwood Street as a base for that operation in Torquay and Paignton.

Negotiations for the purchase by Devon General of the local Timpson's businesses commenced in January 1932. The deal was struck on 7 June, the price £82,500. W. B. Cownie (NEC), F. E. Stanley (NEC), R. H. Nicholls (GWR) and H. A. Short (SR) became directors of the South Devon Motor Garage Co Ltd, and Cownie, Stanley, Nicholls, W. Dennis Thomas and Daniel Campbell (as Manager) became directors of Grey Cars Ltd.

These acquisitions led to the amalgamation of both Grey Cars and Fleet Cars with Devon General proper (a process begun in October 1933) and to the sale of the Primrose Garage property, for £1,550. In another of those 'in house' monetary transfers Grey Cars was 'purchased' for £61,000 and Fleet Cars for . . . £820. The properties transferred to DGO&T from Grey Cars were: Bridge Road garage, Torwood Road garage, 14 East Street in Newton Abbot, 20 Torbay Road, Paignton, 3 Vaughan Parade and 3 Palk Street, 'Chillingworth', Belgrave Road, and 9 Vaughan Parade in Torquay (and 3 Torbay Road, Paignton, as an afterthought in February 1934). From Fleet Cars came 3 Fleet Street, 'The Ruby Hutch', San Remo, Torquay, and a lock-up and office in Torbay Road, Paignton.

Written off in November 1933 were three second-hand Lancias (Nos 104/8/9) and 21 Lancias direct from Fleet Cars, whilst 16 further Lancias taken over from Grey Cars were prepared for sale, just five (Nos 329-33) being retained for further service.

A one-off move in July 1936 was the purchase, for £200, of the coach business run by H. J. Lee of Ottery St Mary. Another surprising action came in March 1937, with the lease to W. Mumford & Sons of Plymouth of lower-floor accommodation at Torwood Street garage, Torquay.

In March 1938 came a decision with far-reaching consequences. Devon General was given an opportunity to acquire Greenslades Tours Ltd of Exeter and Teignmouth, but it was decided that 'in view of the low rate per car mile of the receipts', it was 'improbable that any profit could be made from the business'.

With World War 2 looking ever more likely, that was probably a fair decision at that time.

When war was declared in September 1939 there were plans for the purchase of 10 new coach bodies for the 1931 AEC Ranger chassis acquired from Grey Cars. These were postponed indefinitely, which was just as well, because the following year, still fitted with their original bodies, they went off to serve with the Royal Army Service Corps — and did not return. One of Harold Barnett's last actions as Chairman came in July 1942, when he gave authority for the £25

Like some great limousine, No 339 (AOD 602), a 1936 Leyland Tigress LTB (one of 10), poses in the kind of country it was intended to visit. The bodywork of this petrol-powered 27ft 6in coach was designed and built by Harrington, its canvas roof with back window which retracted into luggage locker making it an ideal vehicle for touring. *Calton Phoenix*

purchase of the 'still alive' goodwill of the excursions and tours business of the late Capt Hutt — by some loophole overlooked back in March 1932. This was simply to safeguard the company's position when conditions would enable a return to this kind of work. Any coaching which took place during what was called 'the duration' was purely for military purposes. In any case, few could have been persuaded that, with the Luftwaffe about, sitting on the top of a Devon hill admiring the view in a pale-grey coach was a very good idea.

In the last few months of the war there was hope that repairs to some 20 coaches lying dormant could be attended to, but these were deferred until the final victory. The latter achieved, Devon General set in motion its plans for the restoration of coaching in March 1946 with the appointment, with effect from 1 April, of Noel Folkard, previously the secretary of the employees pension scheme, as Tours Superintendent — a task he was to perform to everyone's satisfaction until his retirement some 23 years later. Meanwhile the Belgrave Road booking office had been removed from 'Chillingworth' to 'Kistor', in the same road.

At this stage, however, coaches were not the company's top priority, and new ones were not yet on stream. As a stopgap of a

kind not uncommon elsewhere five Leyland Lion TS7 service buses repurchased from the War Department for £60 each were pressed into use as Grey Cars coaches in 1946/7. Although ordered in June 1946, the first dedicated vehicles did not arrive until 1948, in the form of 10 Bedford OBs and 12 AEC Regal IIIs, all bodied by Duple. Also in time for the 1948 season, the lease (held by Devon General since the 'Twenties) was extended on the tours office at 137 Reddenhill Road, Babbacombe.

Grey Cars received its first full-fronted coaches in 1953, with the arrival of a dozen AEC Regal IVs with 41-seat Willowbrook bodywork. The purchase was eased a little by the simultaneous sale at written-down book value — to an associated company, Western Welsh — of the 12 AEC Regal coaches purchased in 1948. Despite the Devon General directors' earlier assessment of Greenslades' worth it did not go unnoticed in October 1953 that BET had purchased that company. The two firms were now overlapping rivals in the same stable. In that spirit of internal competition which BET actively encouraged Devon General reinforced its position in Torquay and Newton Abbot by acquiring first, for £22,500 in the spring of 1954, A. E. Townsend's business of local and extended tours, together with

An extreme shortage of coaches after World War 2 saw eight 'sun saloons' from the bus fleet pressed into service dressed as excursions and tours vehicles. Leyland Tiger TS7 / Harrington 117 (BDV 8) was photographed acting as a 'Grey Car' in Old Road, Tiverton, in August 1952. *Alan B. Cross / Colin Shears collection*

▲ Postwar coaching started in earnest with the arrival of a dozen AEC Regal III 9621A 32-seaters with Duple bodywork built to that firm's much admired A-type design. TCR614 (JOD 614) and its fellow Grey Cars A-types featured an upswept skirt to cope with ferry ramps and Dartmoor bridges. *A. M. Wright / Mallory Saltmarsh collection*

▲ Introduced just before World War 2, the Bedford OB, in its peacetime form, re-emerged afterward as a particularly attractive little vehicle when fitted with 29-seat Duple bodywork. The company ordered 10 in 1948. TCR609 (JUO 609), still in Grey Cars livery, was photographed leaving Paignton for Greenway on service 18. *P. Yeomans / Royston Morgan collection*

TELEPHONE: 87896

Townsend's COACH TOURS

PROPRIETORS:
THE DEVON GENERAL OMNIBUS & TOURING CO. LTD.

Main Booking Office:
147 REDDENHILL ROAD
BABBACOMBE
TORQUAY

its freehold premises at 147 Reddenhill Road, Babbacombe, and seven coaches, the identity of which DGO&T would keep for four seasons; the company also paid £3,000 for a Bedford/Duple Vega coach (TC743) which had been ordered by Townsend. Secondly, in June, it bought from Balls Tours Ltd of Newton Abbot the latter's five coaches, goodwill and assets, for £5,500.

Despite the effects of the Finance Act 1950 upon the spending power of the populace — or perhaps because of it, because they could not yet afford their own means of transport — visitors to Devon still made the tours and excursions market viable, and in February 1957 the company purchased, for £15,000, the four coaches and freehold property of Falkland Garages Ltd of Torquay. The following year there was some dismay in the boardroom as, with effect from 1 April 1958, Wallace Arnold of Leeds acquired Cream Coaches (Torquay) Ltd and Sunbeam Coaches (Torquay) Ltd at a price in excess of what Devon General had been prepared to offer. It was not foreseen at the time that Wallace Arnold Tours (Devon) Ltd, of 16 Torbay Road, Paignton, would outlast by a considerable margin the coaching activities of Devon General.

Perhaps by way of compensation, in April 1958 BET approved the sale to Devon General, for £100, of the

The frowning and awkward-looking bodywork on this Commer Avenger I was built by Heaver in 1951. The driver seems to have had a better view of the world outside from his side windows. No TC748 (MOD 44) was one of a pair of Avengers acquired from Balls Ltd that were repainted in Grey Cars livery. *P. Yeomans / Royston Morgan collection*

▼ On hire to Western/Southern National's 'Royal Blue' — a typical Saturday task for spare Grey Cars coaches — TCR749 (ROD 749) is pictured on a Bournemouth trip. An AEC Reliance MU3RV with 37-seat Weymann 'Fanfare' bodywork, it was one of a pair delivered to Devon General in July 1955. *N. Hamshere / Royston Morgan collection*

▲ Not far to the coach: TCR694 (PDV 694) is parked outside the Grey Cars booking office in Torquay in August 1961. The vehicle is an AEC Regal IV 9822S, one of six with 41-seat Park Royal bodywork built in 1954 to the Devon General company's detailed specification. *Gerald Mead*

One of six Beadle-Commer 'chassisless' 41-seat coaches delivered in 1956, TCC754 (ROD 754) was fitted with the two-stroke TS3 engine. Its unmistakable snarling 'voice' must have echoed nicely off these bleak walls in Dartmoor's Princetown. *Ian Allan Library*

Leading a typically varied convoy of coaches towards London's Victoria Coach Station is Beadle-Commer TCC847 (XTA 847). The six vehicles of this batch — TS3-engined integrals with Beadle 'Rochester' bodywork — were delivered in 1958, after which Beadle returned to more conventional body-on-chassis construction. *Royston Morgan collection*

SEE THE WEST COUNTRY BY THE
GREY CARS
Motor Coach Tours

excursions and tours from Newton Abbot previously operated by Greenslades Tours Ltd. Soon afterwards the company set in motion a major facelift for the booking office at 147 Reddenhill Road, Babbacombe, some £4,650 being set aside for the purpose.

These acquisitions and building upgrades represented the coaching side's reinforcement portfolio until, in June 1966, the Devon General company successfully negotiated with the allied firms of Court Garages (Torquay) Ltd and Bute Court Garages Ltd — the latter operating a self-drive car-hire business, filling station and car-repair garage. This was just the kind of diversification which BET encouraged — but which raised the eyebrows of Devon General's ex-railway (now THC) directors.

Devon General paid £19,483 for Court Garages and £4,030 for Bute Court Garages, which remained autonomous units within the company structure as wholly owned subsidiaries of Devon General. Both did well; by the year ending 30 September 1967 net profits of £2,836 and £1,836 respectively were achieved — a combined return of fractionally under 20% of the cost of acquisition.

However, the sale of BET's road-transport holdings, including the National Electric Construction Co's ordinary stock, to the Transport Holding Company on 1 March 1968, marked the beginning of the end for big-company coaching as we knew it. The National Bus Company was to view the

Delivered (as TCR855) with just a trace of cream around the windows and of dark red on the wings (a 1958/9 style), 855 (XDV 855), a Willowbrook 'Viking'-bodied AEC Reliance, was photographed in later livery on a Royal Blue relief run — a familiar Saturday task for Devon General coaches. *Royston Morgan*

A glorious piece of craftsmanship by any stretch of the imagination, this beautiful coach was an AEC Reliance 2MU3RV with a Willowbrook 41-seat body, delivered in 1961. There were nine coaches in the batch, only two of which, including TCR941 (941 GTA), were built to 8ft width, for extended tours work. *W. Barnes / Philip Platt collection*

89

There were nine vehicles in the 1962 batch of
AEC Reliance 2MU3RV coaches with 41-seat
Willowbrook 'Viscount' bodywork. Here TCR962
(962 HTT) takes a rest from its usual weekly
round of excursions from Torquay and Paignton
to Dartmoor, most parts of which it could reach,
thanks to its 7ft 6in width. *W. Barnes /
Philip Platt collection*

The takeover of Court Garages (Torquay) Ltd in
July 1966, when it became a subsidiary company
of Devon General, was followed by the purchase of
three diesel-engined Bedford SB5 coaches with
41-seat Duple Bella Vega bodywork. They operated
in Court Garages colours, as demonstrated by
CXF 256G. *Philip Platt collection*

Followed appropriately by a
Black & White coach from
Cheltenham, No 32 (HOD 32E)
heads for the Gloucestershire
spa town, on hire to Associated
Motorways. This 36-footer,
delivered in 1967, was bodied by
Duple (Northern) Ltd at a time
when coachbuilders generally
were about to abandon
curvaceous side elevations.
Royston Morgan

excursions, tours and private-hire business with disfavour — others could do that!

Thus on 1 April 1969 G. K. Metcalf, Greenslades' Engineer, took on that role also for Devon General's vehicles. Over the years many tired Grey Cars had been cascaded to Greenslades; now two were 'transferred'. In October 1969 Grey Cars' excursion work from Tiverton was sold for a song (£500) to the local firm of Kingdom's Tours, whilst on the 17th of that month the Devon General board, in obedient fashion, 'approved' the replacement of the traditional Grey Cars livery with what, mercifully, proved to be a short-lived 'South West Area' coach livery. In Devon General's case this took the ghostly form of a horizontal grey band around an otherwise overall white.

By the time the grey band (and the blue one for Royal Blue and the green for Greenslades) had disappeared from the coaches Devon General's June 1970 order for five Plaxton-bodied Bristol LH coaches had been cancelled and the Court Garages and Bute Court subsidiaries 'transferred' to Devon General proper, for the 'in house' sum of £11,431, ready for sale.

On 17 December 1970 it was announced that the Grey Cars operation was to be transferred to Greenslades. It was the end of a very long era — but not quite the end of the famous 'Grey Cars' name, as revealed overleaf...

A 36ft AEC Reliance 2U3RA with 49-seat Harrington Grenadier coachwork, 26 (EOD 26D) leaves its base in Torquay, running light to Paignton to pick up booked passengers for an excursion, possibly to Plymouth — always a popular destination for tourists with a taste for Britain's naval history. *Royston Morgan*

On Friday 17 October 1969 the board members of Devon General sat and formally 'approved' a new colour scheme for Grey Cars coaches — one imposed upon them by the National Bus Company. Included that we might make our own judgement is this photograph of Reliance/Grenadier EOD 25D in Exeter bus station in June 1970. *Royston Morgan*

The cliff cable railway between Babbacombe and Oddicombe Beach still carries holidaymakers down its perfectly straight track towards the waves more than 720ft below. Although built by Torquay Corporation it was for nine years (1926-35) worked by the Torquay Tramways Co Ltd.
Colin Morris

The Grey Cars fleetname was resurrected in 1987 by a small group of ex-company drivers using leased vehicles. The famous name subsequently passed to a Newton Abbot-based firm, one of whose Volvo/Van Hool coaches is seen in Higher Downs Road, Babbacombe, in May 2005.
Colin Morris

▶ To conclude the tale of the company number begun at the very start of this story: When the National Bus Company was itself broken up into saleable bits by the Thatcher Government, those privatised pieces became new companies in their own right, with newly issued company numbers — Devon General Ltd being an example. One or two, however, received instead those of long-established operating companies which had not been officially wound up but underwent an appropriate change of name.

▼ As the privatisation process advanced, the late John Birks, to his eternal credit, ensured that the minute books of many ex-NBC subsidiaries were preserved. Most went to the Kithead Trust at Droitwich, in whose foundation John played a leading part. The team at Kithead, wondering what had happened to the Devon General records, searched as far afield as Salisbury — without result. Eventually a parcel labelled 'Crosville Wales' arrived at Kithead and was opened. It contained . . . guess what! The chronological records of Company No 155374, The Devon General Omnibus & Touring Co Ltd, starting on 22 May 1919! I am honoured to have been granted access to them.

A remarkable collection of ex-Devon General vehicles beautifully restored by resolute individual members of the Devon General Society including, in particular, Philip Platt, Colin Shears, Royston Morgan, Bob Follwell, Ron Greet and members of the Blackman family. *Philip Platt*

A plaque erected outside a housing development where once stood the St Marychurch depot of the Torquay Tramways Co Ltd. In the modern manner the name isn't quite right, but the dates are correct — and the gesture is warming. *Colin Morris*

The great man himself. On Sunday 31 May 1992 Tom Strange, the last General Manager of 'proper' Devon General, returned from his retirement for a Society celebration at Oldway Mansion, Paignton. Here he poses with Philip Platt's beautiful 'Cavalier' 1 RDV as his daughter, Stella Gardner, chats with the late and much-missed Gerald Truran. *Royston Morgan*

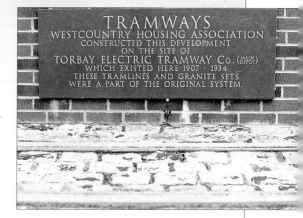

TRAMWAYS
WESTCOUNTRY HOUSING ASSOCIATION
CONSTRUCTED THIS DEVELOPMENT
ON THE SITE OF
TORBAY ELECTRIC TRAMWAY Co. (MAIN DEPOT)
WHICH EXISTED HERE 1907 - 1934
THESE TRAMLINES AND GRANITE SETS
WERE A PART OF THE ORIGINAL SYSTEM.

Two AEC Reliance coaches on a visit to Buckfast Abbey — a 'must' for tourists. Both have coachwork by Willowbrook; the 'Viscount' style of TCR960 (960 HTT) had supplanted the earlier 'Viking' on TCR890 (890 ADV), whose dark-red stripes, added in 1962, did little to relieve the 'bleary-eyed' frontal appearance. *Royston Morgan collection*

What appeared to be the end of an era came in December 1970, when it was decided to subsume the Grey Cars name under that of Greenslades Tours Ltd. It was later to re-emerge, however. Meanwhile, Philip Platt's restored Reliance recalls 'the real thing'. *Royston Morgan*

▲ Lovingly restored and posing beside the ancient Drewe Arms in the village of Drewsteignton, AEC Regal/Weymann SR510 (HUO 510) recreates a journey on service 29 from Exeter to Moretonhampstead — not quite the longest name in Devon, but very nearly. *Gerald Truran*

The quintessential image of beautiful Torquay forms a backdrop for immaculately turned-out preserved AEC Regent V/Metro-Cammell 524 (EOD 524D). pausing on the climb from Meadfoot Beach at Hesketh Crescent, long considered a jewel of local architecture. *Royston Morgan*

The shining! Photographed at the centre of things during the Devon General Society's celebration of the company's 65th anniversary is DR585 (KOD 585). New in 1949, this Weymann-bodied AEC Regent III is the beautifully restored property of Ron Greet and was in truly sparkling form when photographed inside Newton Road depot. Its 7ft 6in width is a reminder of BET's campaign, 'We are trying to get you a wider seat'. In this it was successful; Philip Platt's DR661, new just three years later, is 8ft wide! *Philip Platt*

Posed outside Sidmouth garage, apparently ready for a journey on the service to Newton Poppleford and Exeter, is the appropriately numbered 9 (9 RDV), an AEC Reliance 2U3RA with 53-seat bodywork by Marshall, delivered in 1964. *Royston Morgan*

Preserved AEC Regent V 524 poses beneath the arches as a Great Western tank engine of the Paignton & Dartmouth steam railway passes overhead with a train of holidaymakers bound for Kingswear — and a trip across the River Dart, most likely. *Royston Morgan*

Bibliography

Publications found helpful in the compilation of this volume and/or recommended for further reading are:

Books
Aish, Norman: *South Western Buses in Camera* (Ian Allan, 1977)
Barham, Fisher: *Torbay Transport* (Glasney Press, Falmouth, 1979)
Cummings, John: *Railway Motor Buses and Bus Services in the British Isles 1902-1933* Vol 2 (OPC, 1980)
Folkard, Leslie F.: *History of Devon General* (Ian Allan, 1966)
Folkard, Leslie, and Platt, Philip: *Devon General — a pictorial history* (Roundoak Publishing, 1994)
Fulford, Roger: *The Sixth Decade, 1946-1956* (BET, 1956)
Gentry, P. W.: *Tramways of the West of England* (LRTL, 1952/1960)
Kelsey, Malcolm, and Gray, Paul: *British Bus Celebration* (Capital Transport, 1986)
Sambourne, Roy C.: *Exeter: a Century of Public Transport* (Glasney Press, Falmouth, 1976)

House magazines
Devon General: *Magazine of Movement and Mirth — the official record of our deeds and misdeeds* (1932 onwards)
Devon General Staff News (1946 onwards)

Journals
DG Digest — the Devon General Society magazine
Publications by the West Country Historic Omnibus & Transport Trust
Numerous articles in *Buses Illustrated* and *Buses* by Ian Allan Publishing

Contact details
Devon General Society website: www.devongeneral.org.uk
WHOTT website: www.busmuseum.org.uk
Readers wishing to learn more about independent operators in the Devon General area or in other parts of the West Country are referred to a series of booklets published by Roger Grimley, details of which can be obtained from: Old Post, Bigbury, Kingsbridge, Devon TQ7 4AP